Evidence
2010–2011

Routledge
Taylor & Francis Group

LONDON AND NEW YORK

Sixth edition published 2010
by Routledge
2 Park Square, Milton Park, Abingdon, Oxon OX14 4RN

Simultaneously published in the USA and Canada
by Routledge
270 Madison Avenue, New York, NY 10016

Routledge is an imprint of the Taylor & Francis Group, an informa business

© 2006, 2008, 2010 Routledge

Previous editions published by Cavendish Publishing Limited
First edition   1997
Second edition   1999
Third edition   2002
Fourth edition   2004
Fifth edition   2008

Typeset in Rotis Sans by RefineCatch Limited, Bungay, Suffolk
Printed and bound in Great Britain by TJ International Ltd, Padstow, Cornwall

British Library Cataloguing in Publication Data
A catalogue record for this book is available from the British Library

Library of Congress Control Number: 2009912624

ISBN10: 0-415-56664-9 (pbk)
ISBN13: 978-0-415-56664-3 (pbk)

ISBN10: 0-203-85821-2 (eBook)
ISBN13: 978-0-203-85821-9 (eBook)

Contents

Table of Cases

Table of Statutes

Table of Statutory Instruments

Table of European Legislation

How to use this book

Welcome to this new edition of Routledge Evidence Lawcards. In response to student feedback, we've added some new features to these new editions to give you all the support and preparation you need in order to face your law exams with confidence.

Inside this book you will find:

■ NEW tables of cases and statutes for ease of reference

■ Revision Checklists

We've summarised the key topics you will need to know for your law exams and broken them down into a handy revision checklist. Check them out at the beginning of each chapter, then after you have the chapter down, revisit the checklist and tick each topic off as you gain knowledge and confidence.

1

Sources of law

Primary legislation: Acts of Parliament	☐
Secondary legislation	☐
Case law	☐
System of precedent	☐
Common law	☐
Equity	☐
EU law	☐
Human Rights Act 1998	☐

■ Key Cases

We've identified the key cases that are most likely to come up in exams. To help you to ensure that you can cite cases with ease, we've included a brief account of the case and judgment for a quick aide-memoire.

HENDY LENNOX v GRAHAME PUTTICK [1984]

Basic facts

Diesel engines were supplied, subject to a *Romalpa* clause, then fitted to generators. Each engine had a serial number. When the buyer became insolvent the seller sought to recover one engine. The Receiver argued that the process of fitting the engine to the generator passed property to the buyer. The court disagreed and allowed the seller to recover the still identifiable engine despite the fact that some hours of work would be required to disconnect it.

Relevance

If the property remains identifiable and is not irredeemably changed by the manufacturing process a *Romalpa* clause may be viable.

■ Companion Website

At the end of each chapter you will be prompted to visit the Routledge Evidence Lawcards companion website where you can test your understanding online with specially prepared multiple-choice questions, as well as revise the key terms with our online glossary.

You should now be confident that you would be able to tick all of the boxes on the checklist at the beginning of this chapter. To check your knowledge of Sources of law why not visit the companion website and take the Multiple Choice Question test. Check your understanding of the terms and vocabulary used in this chapter with the flashcard glossary.

■ Exam Practice

Once you've acquired the basic knowledge, you'll want to put it to the test. The Routledge Questions and Answers provides examples of the kinds of questions that you will face in your exams, together with suggested answer plans and a fully-worked model answer. We've included one example free at the end of this book to help you put your technique and understanding into practice.

QUESTION 1

What are the main sources of law today?

Answer plan

This is, apparently, a very straightforward question, but the temptation is to ignore the European Community (EU) as a source of law and to over-emphasise custom as a source. The following structure does not make these mistakes:

■ in the contemporary situation, it would not be improper to start with the EU as a source of UK law;

■ then attention should be moved on to domestic sources of law: statute and common law;

■ the increased use of delegated legislation should be emphasised;

■ custom should be referred to, but its extremely limited operation must be emphasised.

ANSWER

European law

Since the UK joined the European Economic Community (EEC), now the EU, it has progressively but effectively passed the power to create laws which are operative in this country to the wider European institutions. The UK is now subject to Community law, not just as a direct consequence of the various treaties of accession passed by the UK Parliament, but increasingly, it is subject to the secondary legislation generated by the various institutions of the EU.

1

Relevance, admissibility and weight

BASIC CONCEPTS

DEFINITION OF 'EVIDENCE'

The meaning of 'evidence' depends to some extent on context, but the word is often used to refer to any matter of fact, the effect, tendency or design of which is to produce in the mind a persuasion of the existence or non-existence of some other matter of fact.

In a practical sense, evidence is material presented to the court in order to persuade the fact-finder (judge and/or jury) of the probability of a particular fact.

The law of evidence commonly deals with issues of:

- How evidence has been obtained

- How evidence is adduced at the trial

- How evidence can be used by the fact-finder

- How the fact-finder should evaluate the evidence.

At one extreme of evidential theory is for the court to admit all relevant evidence and leave issues of weight and probative value to the fact-finder to decide when making its deliberations. This is the notion of free proof and was advocated by Jeremy Bentham. Most states, however, take a much narrower view of the evidence that can be admitted at trial, and so the law of evidence becomes concerned with rules of admissibility (or rather exclusionary rules). Many of the rules of admissibility of evidence, therefore, take the form of a general exclusionary rule with a number of exceptions allowing admissibility under certain conditions. The general rules of exclusion tend to concern particular categories of evidence that are deemed to be too prejudicial for the defendant or witness. Some rules of admissibility include a judicial discretion to admit the evidence, or require a warning of caution to be given to the jury in how they should handle that particular piece of evidence or evaluate it, or may involve an evaluation of the other evidence in the case before that piece of evidence can be admitted.

Consequently, not all evidence is admissible. The law of evidence determines if a relevant piece of evidence will ultimately be admissible and what the fact-finder can use that evidence to prove.

Where the law creates a rule of exclusion for a particular type of evidence (eg hearsay) it is important to understand why that rule has evolved. The answer will usually be because that particular type of evidence has a tendency to be unreliable, and hence the fact-finder may place too much weight on the evidence when it does not warrant it. A second common reason for exclusionary rules is prejudicial effect, meaning that the revelation of that piece of evidence to the fact-finder (eg jury) may cause it to pre-judge the issue of guilt, for example if the jury knew the defendant had previous criminal convictions for very similar offences. The law of evidence also follows other areas of the law in restricting the admission of evidence on the basis of public policy. For example, the exclusion of confessions obtained by force is a rule of public policy, as well, of course, as human rights.

HUMAN RIGHTS AND THE LAW OF EVIDENCE

Naturally, since the enactment of the 1998 Human Rights Act, a rights-based approach has been taken to issues of admissibility of evidence. The main focus for the law of evidence within the European Convention on Human Rights is Article 6 governing the right to a fair trial, which concerns both civil and criminal cases. There is also Article 3 prohibiting torture or inhuman or degrading treatment or punishment, Article 5 concerning the right to liberty and security of the person, particularly detention, and Article 8 concerning respect for private and family life.

Article 6 applies even before trial and so can cover issues such as the way in which evidence was collected. Note the following key provisions:

- Article 6(1) stipulates that 'everyone is entitled to a fair and public hearing within a reasonable time by an independent and impartial tribunal established by law'.

- Article 6(2) stipulates the principle of innocence until proven guilty.

- Article 6(3) includes the aspects of legal advice and the examination of witnesses giving evidence against the Defendant.

The European Court of Human Rights has built up a large body of case law governing Article 6. The general approach of the Court towards the law of evidence in a given Member State is not to issue specific rules of admissibility but to ensure that in a given case the right to a fair trial was not breached. Inevitably these rulings have impacted on the design of admissibility laws within the Member States.

> ### ▶ TEIXEIRA DE CASTRO v PORTUGAL [1998]
>
> #### Basic facts
> Undercover officers in anti-drug trafficking operations in Portugal encouraged the defendant to procure drugs for them. The question was whether the officers had acted as 'agents provocateurs', in inducing the defendant to commit an offence he would not otherwise have committed.
>
> #### Relevance
> Finding a violation of Article 6(1) the Court held, 'The admissibility of evidence is primarily a matter for regulation by national law and as a general rule it is for the national courts to assess the evidence before them. The Court's task under the Convention is not to give a ruling as to whether statements of witnesses were properly admitted as evidence, but rather to ascertain whether the proceedings as a whole, including the way in which evidence was taken, were fair.'

EVIDENTIAL FORMS

ORAL OR TESTIMONIAL EVIDENCE

This is evidence spoken orally during the trial but does not necessarily require a 'live' performance. Video-recorded witness statements are often presented in court as a witness' evidence, and similarly evidence can be given via 'live link' from another room in the court. In some situations testimonial evidence need not be oral at all, but written. For example, in civil cases witnesses will usually give their evidence in writing (see the Civil Procedure Rules 1998). Most witnesses will present their oral testimony under oath of affirmation but some do not, particularly child witnesses. A witness may give oral evidence of events that he has seen, or heard, or of which he has acquired knowledge. Examples include the oral testimony of a witness to having seen the defendant shoot the victim, or having seen the defendant in a particular location, or having heard screams.

DOCUMENTARY EVIDENCE

This is evidence in written or recorded form (eg film or tape) which is used as evidence of its contents. A 'document' is defined as 'anything in which information of any description is recorded' (s 134 of the Criminal Justice Act 2003, and s 13 of the Civil Evidence Act 1995). Examples include, a surveillance video which shows the defendant punching the victim, a will or contract, or telephone/computer records.

REAL EVIDENCE

This is evidence that is physically produced in court so that its nature can be inspected. Examples include weapons, the fact that the defendant is left-handed, a blood-stained document, items of clothing, photographs of the crime scene, and the demeanour of a witness whilst giving oral evidence. If the thing to be inspected cannot be brought into the court because it is too big, for example a house, the judge and jury may be required to view the evidence by visiting it. The evidence gathered during the visit to the location will then form part of the evidence in the case.

HEARSAY EVIDENCE

Hearsay is defined in ss 114 and 115 of the 2003 Criminal Justice Act to mean a statement, not made in oral evidence in the proceedings, that is relied on as evidence of a matter stated in it (note s 121 refers to a more limited meaning of hearsay for the purposes of multiple hearsay and excludes statements made in previous court proceedings from the scope of inadmissible hearsay). Essentially what is excluded is testimony that recounts a statement made either by the witness himself or by another person made sometime before the trial where that statement is being adduced to prove that what the person said was true. An example would be where witness A told witness B that she saw the defendant shoot the victim. It would be hearsay for Witness B to recount to the court that witness A had told her that he had seen the shooting by the defendant because what is being relied upon is the truth of that fact: that the defendant shot the victim.

ORIGINAL EVIDENCE

Again original evidence involves statements made by witnesses out of court, but the evidence is original (and not hearsay) when the statement is relied upon for a purpose other than establishing its truth. Non-hearsay purposes of statements would be where the witness sought only to rely on the fact that the statement was made, or was made in a particular way or at a particular time. Examples include, statements made at the time of signing a contract, or statements used to prove libel.

DIRECT EVIDENCE
This is evidence which goes directly to the proof of a fact in issue. An example would be where a witness gave evidence that she saw the defendant kill the victim. Depending on the context this evidence can also refer to evidence perceived with a witness' own senses, as opposed to hearsay evidence.

CIRCUMSTANTIAL EVIDENCE
This is evidence of a fact that is not itself a fact in issue, but is a fact from which the existence or non-existence of a fact in issue can be inferred. Circumstantial evidence operates indirectly by tending to prove a fact relevant to the issue. An example would be gun shot residue found on the defendant; while it does not prove that he shot the victim it does evidence that he shot a gun and by inference that it was the victim. Other examples would involve evidence that demonstrated motive, opportunity and preparatory acts to commit the crime. A conviction can be secured on circumstantial evidence alone.

OPINION EVIDENCE
Ordinary witnesses are not allowed to give their opinion, they must only testify to facts personally perceived. Expert witnesses may, however, give opinion evidence on issues within their expertise and beyond the court's competence.

BEST EVIDENCE RULE
This rule probably no longer exists but required the best form of evidence to be given if available, for example the original version of a document rather than a copy.

RELEVANCE, WEIGHT AND ADMISSIBILITY

To be adduced in court an item of evidence must be both relevant and admissible.

ALL evidence must be   Relevant + Admissible

Relevant evidence can be made inadmissible by

1   A rule of evidence excluding that type of evidence, or
2   Judicial discretion to exclude the evidence (either at common law or under statute).

The first question you must ask, therefore, is whether the evidence is relevant.

RELEVANCE

'Relevance' refers to the relationship that exists between an item of evidence and a fact that has to be proved, which makes the matter requiring proof more or less probable. In the vast majority of cases, it is not the law that determines whether an item of evidence is relevant, but logic and general experience. General experience will often be expressed as a generalisation about the way things are in the world. While it is not a question of law, the issue of relevance will be a decision for the judge and if relevance is disputed in a criminal case the judge will hear evidence on this in what is known as a voir dire (or trial within a trial), which takes place without the jury. The classic definition of relevance is provided by Lord Simon of Glaisdale in *DPP v Kilbourne* [1973]:

'Evidence is relevant if it is logically probative of some matter which requires proof . . . It is sufficient to say . . . that relevant (i.e. logically probative or disprobative) evidence is evidence which makes the matter which requires proof more or less probable.'

Evidence will be relevant if it makes the fact to be proved or disproved that little bit more likely. Evidence which does not make the fact more or less likely will add nothing to the case by way of proof, and so is irrelevant. The burden is on the party who tenders evidence to show its relevance; it is not for the party challenging relevance to show that the evidence in question is irrelevant (*R v Bracewell* [1978]). Relevance is important for the law of evidence because:

■ irrelevant evidence is inadmissible (*R v Turner* [1975]);

■ the way in which an item of evidence is relevant may govern its admissibility (eg, hearsay, similar fact evidence).

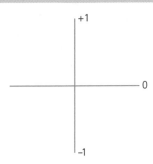

The probability or otherwise of what one party to litigation alleges can be expressed in the diagram above. The point +1 represents the mental condition of being certain that what the party alleges is true; −1 represents certainty that the allegation is untrue. Any item of evidence making it more or less likely that the allegation is true will have a place on the scale at some point between 0 and +1, or between 0 and −1, and will, in principle, be relevant at trial. Note that an item of evidence does not have to be conclusive to be relevant.

Questions of relevance generally depend on the individual circumstances of each case (*R v Guney* [1998]). But a judge may decide that something that is relevant according to ordinary reasoning is not legally relevant. This may be the case, for example, where a judge wishes to avoid a proliferation of side issues that may confuse a jury, cause delay or give rise to mere speculation (*Hollingham v Head* [1858]; *R v Blastland* [1986]).

▶ R v BLASTLAND [1986]

Basic facts

The defendant admitted buggery but denied murder. The defendant sought to evidence witnesses to statements by a man, Mark, who had told several people in an excitable manner of the boy's murder before that fact had become public knowledge (and who had confessed to the murder).

Relevance

The House of Lords viewed the evidence of Mark's statements as showing Mark's state of mind, but went on to hold Mark's state of mind as irrelevant to the facts in issue. It was not what Mark knew but how he knew it and it was mere speculation to suggest that the knowledge was due to his murdering the boy. (See Chapter 8, 'Confessions'.)

RELEVANT TO WHAT?

To constitute relevant evidence it must relate to the three evidential matters to be proven:

(a) Facts in issue

(b) Collateral facts

(c) Evidentiary facts (background facts).

Facts in issue are those facts which the party must prove in order to succeed in the claim; they relate to the substantive legal requirements to make out the offence or civil claim. For example, in criminal law all the elements of the offence to prove that the defendant is guilty. In civil claims, this expression refers to those facts alleged in the statements of case, including facts necessary to establish defences that are either denied or not admitted by the other party.

Collateral facts refer to matters going to the admissibility or weight of evidence used to prove the primary facts in issue, such as facts relating to the competence of a witness to testify, or the witness' credibility, or facts which affect the admissibility of any evidence (eg that a confession was obtained in circumstances of undue pressure).

Evidence of facts surrounding an event are often admitted in order to show the context in which words were spoken or events occurred.

WEIGHT

The 'weight' of an item of evidence refers to the extent to which that item makes a proposition more or less probable. In the diagram above, it is relevance that gets an item of evidence onto the scale in the first place, but it is weight that governs the position that it takes there. The 'weightier' the evidence, the nearer it will be to one or other extremity. Where the judicial function is split between a judge and a jury, questions of relevance are decided by the judge, and questions of weight by the jury. But a judge sometimes makes decisions about weight, for example, where the defence asks that an item of prosecution evidence be excluded on the ground that its prejudicial effect outweighs its probative value.

Although relevance and weight are distinct concepts, there is some connection between them, because the weight of an item of evidence may be affected by the form of the generalisation that is relied on to support its relevance. The bolder the generalisation, the weightier the evidence is likelier to be. But a bold generalisation is less likely than a cautious one to be true. So where X is charged with the murder of Y, and it can be proved that X quarrelled with Y shortly before the latter's death, the relevance and weight of the fact of the quarrel might be considered in the table below.

Generalisation	Comment
(1) People who quarrel with others usually murder them	If true, the evidence is relevant and weighty. But this generalisation is certainly false, and, unless a more acceptable generalisation can be found, the evidence must be irrelevant
(2) Where a murder victim has quarrelled recently with someone, that person is more likely to be the culprit than someone who had not quarrelled recently with him	A little more plausible. If true, the evidence is relevant and fairly weighty
(3) Where a murder victim has recently had a quarrel with someone, that person may have had a motive for murder, and may be more likely to be the culprit than someone who had no motive	Probably an acceptable generalisation, so the evidence of the quarrel is relevant, but it is too weak to be anything more than of very slight weight

ADMISSIBILITY

An item of evidence may be relevant and weighty, but inadmissible because of some rule of law. Admissibility is a question of law and decisions about admissibility are made by the judge.

FUNCTIONS OF JUDGE AND JURY

In jury trials, the judicial function is divided between the judge, whose decision on matters of law is (subject to a right of appeal) final, and the jury, who are in principle the sole judges of fact. Every summing up should contain a direction to the jury about these separate functions (*R v Jackson* [1992]). It is particularly important that the division of functions be made clear to the jury, because the law permits the trial judge to comment on the evidence in his summing up (*R v Sparrow* [1973]), although the judge should not go so far as to give his own views about whether or not a witness has told the truth (*R v Iroegbu* [1988]).

But note that a judge in a criminal trial may have to make rulings about facts, for example:

- where it is necessary to establish the existence of certain facts (such as those required to establish a witness' competence to testify, or the admissibility of a confession) before a particular witness' evidence, or a particular item of evidence, can be admitted;

- where the defence submits that there is no case to answer (*R v Galbraith* [1981]);

- where evidence is said to be contaminated for the purposes of s 107 of the Criminal Justice Act 2003.

Although the judge's directions on the law are his responsibility, it has become increasingly common for judges to invite prosecution and defence advocates to address them on the content of those directions where there is room for more than one view about what they should be. Thus, in *R v Higgins* [1995], the Court of Appeal suggested that counsel has a duty to raise appropriate matters before closing speeches without waiting to be asked by the judge.

In *R v N* [1998], the Court of Appeal observed that it had frequently said that difficulties would be avoided, and cases conducted with clarity, if discussion took place between judge and counsel at the end of the evidence about points of law and, more particularly, about the points of evidence that had arisen. (Such discussion should, of course, be in open court, but in the absence of the jury.)

DISCLOSURE

Before a civil or criminal case gets to court there are obligations on the parties of disclosure, essentially an obligation for the parties to reveal their case and hence for the main issues of contention to come to light. In civil cases pre-trial disclosure takes place when the claimant files the claim form which indicates the nature of the case, the defendant will then serve their statement in response to that claim. In sum, and according to Part 31 of the Civil Procedure Rules 1998, the parties exchange lists of documents in their possession, on which they rely or which support another party's case.

For criminal cases the police must appoint a disclosure officer who must record and retain all information and material gathered or generated during the investigation. The prosecution has an obligation to disclose information to the defence under (the recently amended) s 3 of the Criminal Procedure and Investigations Act 1996, but disclosure here is a preparation for trial and so is only where the defendant is to be tried on indictment. Section 7A places a continuing duty of disclosure on the prosecution until the final result in the case (acquittal, conviction, etc). Under the new s 3 test the prosecutor must disclose to the defence any material that might reasonably be considered capable of undermining the prosecution case or of assisting the case for the defence. The defendant also has an obligation of disclosure to provide a defence statement, indicating the nature of his defence. Section 6A of the Criminal Procedure and Investigations Act 1996 defines a 'defence statement' as a 'written statement (a) setting out the nature of the accused's defence, including any particular defences on which he intends to rely, (b) indicating the matters of fact on which he takes issue with the prosecution, (c) setting out, in the case of each such matter, why he takes issue with the prosecution, (ca) setting out particulars of the matters of fact on which he intends to rely for the purposes of his defence, and (d) indicating any point of law (including any point as to the admissibility of evidence or an abuse of process) which he wishes to take, and any authority on which he intends to rely for that purpose.'

A defendant wishing to rely on an alibi should disclose this, including the name, address and date of birth of the person (s 6A(2) Criminal Procedure and Investigations Act 1996).

You should now be confident that you would be able to tick all of the boxes on the checklist at the beginning of this chapter. To check your knowledge of Relevance, admissibility and weight why not visit the companion website and take the Multiple Choice Question test. Check your understanding of the terms and vocabulary used in this chapter with the flashcard glossary.

2

Burden of proof

BURDEN OF PROOF

The 'burden of proof' is the obligation which rests on a party to prove a particular fact in a civil or criminal case and which must be 'discharged' or 'satisfied' if that party is to win on the issue in question. This burden is often referred to as the 'legal' or 'persuasive' burden, but must be distinguished from the *evidential burden*.

Students are often confused by the two notions of legal burden (sometimes referred to as 'the persuasive burden') and evidential burden. The legal burden requires the party to prove a particular fact in issue to the relevant standard of proof (beyond reasonable doubt, for example). If the standard of proof is not met the party will not have proven that particular fact in issue.

The so-called evidential burden, on the other hand, is not strictly a burden at all. It is best seen as a rule of common sense, which says that there must be some evidence for a particular issue to become a live one, to be fit for consideration by the jury or some other tribunal of fact. In this sense, the court will talk of 'raising an issue' (*Jayasena v R* [1970]). The judge will decide if the matter has been sufficiently raised by the evidence (satisfied the evidential burden).

Put simply for all facts in issue and any defences/counter claims, unless the parties agree otherwise, some evidence must be adduced (the evidential burden). How much evidence needs to be adduced for a particular fact in issue or defence/counter claim will depend on whether that fact carries a legal burden of proof, and ultimately which party bears the burden (since the prosecution have a higher standard of proof than that defence).

THE LEGAL BURDEN OF PROOF IN CIVIL CASES

In civil cases the allocation of the legal burden has generally occurred over centuries via case law and statute. In a case of negligence, for example, the claimant would bear the legal burden to prove all the elements of negligence (duty of care was owed, breach of duty, etc), while the defendant will bear the legal burden to prove contributory negligence, if pleaded.

Otherwise, the general guiding principle is that the burden of proof lies with the party that asserts a fact in issue – either in the claim or defence. Note especially the *dicta* of Viscount Maugham in *Constantine (Joseph) ss Line Ltd v* *Imperial Smelting* [1942]:

■ the burden should lie on the party who affirms a proposition, rather than on the party who denies it (but the courts avoid a mechanical approach to the 'affirmation or denial' test).

In other words, where the burden of proof should rest is merely a question of policy and fairness based on experience in the different situations (*Rustad v Great Northern Rly Co* [1913]). In looking at those situations, a court will be concerned with, amongst other things, the ease with which a party may be able to discharge a burden of proof. See, for example, the following cases.

The Glendarroch [1894]

In a contract for the carriage of goods by sea, the shippers were exempt from liability for damage caused by perils of the sea, unless the damage was due to their own negligence. The goods were damaged when the ship became stranded.

Held: the owners of the goods asserting the claim had to prove the existence of the contract and non-delivery. In order to rely on the exception to liability, the shippers had to show that the loss was caused by perils of the sea. It was then for the owners of the goods to establish the exception to that exception by proving that the shippers had been negligent.

Constantine (Joseph) ss Line Ltd v Imperial Smelting [1942]

Frustration was pleaded by shipowners as a defence to a claim by charterers.

Held: it was not necessary for the shipowners to prove that the frustrating event had occurred without fault on their part. The burden was on the charterers to prove negligence by the shipowners so as to bar them from relying on frustration.

Levison v Patent Steam Carpet Cleaning Co [1978]

The defendant cleaners relied on an exclusion clause when goods sent to them for cleaning were lost. This clause would not assist them if they had been guilty of a fundamental breach of contract.

Held: it was for the cleaners to prove that they had not been guilty of fundamental breach and not for the customer to prove that they had.

THE LEGAL BURDEN OF PROOF IN CRIMINAL CASES

> Refer back to Article 6(2) – In a criminal case the accused is presumed innocent.
>
> This is one way of saying that the prosecution must prove the case against the accused, including any *mens rea* requirement.

In *Woolmington v DPP* [1935] the basic rule was laid down by Viscount Sankey in the House of Lords:

> Throughout the web of English criminal law one golden thread is always to be seen, that it is the duty of the prosecution to prove the prisoner's guilt.

Thus, in criminal cases the basic rule is that the prosecution bear the legal burden on each fact in issue. If the prosecution fails to prove a particular fact in issue the defendant will be acquitted. The prosecution must also *disprove* any defence raised by the accused.

Viscount Sankey did, however, suggest that this golden rule was subject to exceptions in the case of the defence of insanity, and subject also to any statutory exception, which may expressly or impliedly impose a legal burden of proof on the defendant (often referred to as the 'reverse onus' since it lies on the defendant). Ordinarily then the defendant will only bear an evidential burden to bring evidence to counter prosecution evidence and to raise his defence, for example of alibi. With regard to certain exceptional defences, however, the defendant will in fact bear a legal burden to prove that defence. When a legal burden is imposed on the defendant to prove a particular defence, he must prove that defence to the requisite defence standard of proof which is the balance of probabilities. But it must be noted that if he fails to prove the exceptional defence to the requisite standard he will not be able to rely on that defence and he will often, therefore, be convicted. The issue of legal burdens is a very controversial area of the law and has generated much case law from the European Court of Human Rights, due to the question of compatibility of such defence legal burdens with the presumption of innocence under Article 6 of the European Convention on Human Rights.

Two questions thus arise:

1   Does the statute/offence impose a legal burden on the defendant to prove a particular fact?

2   If so, is the imposition of that legal burden compatible with Article 6?

There is no problem in seeing where the burdens lie if a statute provides, for example, that an accused person shall be guilty of an offence 'unless the contrary is proved' (s 2 of the Prevention of Corruption Act 1916). The question whether Parliament in any given case has *impliedly* overruled *Woolmington*, however, is more difficult to resolve.

▶ WOOLMINGTON v DPP [1935]

Basic facts

The accused was charged with murdering his estranged wife. He admitted shooting her but claimed that he had threatened to shoot himself unless she returned to him and had shot her by accident. The trial judge directed the jury that once it was established that the victim had died as a result of the defendant's act, he had the burden of proving that it was an accident rather than an intentional killing. Clearly, the trial judge placed the burden of proving the lack of *mens rea* on the defendant. The House of Lords held this to be a misdirection and Viscount Sankey laid down the basic rule.

Relevance

This case laid down the basic rule regarding the presumption of innocence for all criminal cases and the onus on the prosecution to prove all facts in issue, including *mens rea*.

The common law defence of insanity (to murder) imposes a legal burden on the defendant to prove that insanity (*M'Naghten's Case* [1843]); where 'To establish a defence on the grounds of insanity it must be clearly proved by the defendant that at the time of the committing of the act the accused was labouring under such a defect of reason, from disease of the mind, as not to know the nature and quality of the act he was doing; or, if he did know it, that he did not know that what he was doing was wrong.'

The standard of proof on the defendant is that of the balance of probabilities. Some explain the reverse onus on the basis that it is too difficult for the prosecution to have to prove sanity, while others suggest that it follows from the basic maxim in English law that all men are presumed sane and so it is for him to prove otherwise. The defence of diminished responsibility, s 2(2) of the Homicide Act has been upheld as imposing a legal burden in Lambert (see below).

In addition, defence legal burdens (reverse onus) are also allocated by s 101 of the Magistrates' Courts Act 1980. According to s 101, where the defendant relies for his defence on any 'exception, exemption, proviso, excuse or qualification', whether or not it is part of the description of the offence, the burden of proving such a defence shall be on him. For clarification, in *R v Edwards* [1975], the Court of Appeal held that this principle was not confined to cases heard in the Magistrates' Courts; the provision was a statutory statement of a common law rule applicable in all criminal courts.

The reasoning for reverse onuses in these circumstances was that where there is a minor regulatory offence, usually where an act is prohibited subject to specified classes of persons or with specified qualifications or with license/ permission, it will be easier for the defendant to prove that license etc rather than for the prosecution to have to prove the non-existence to the defendant of the long list of exceptions (eg no license). But defence legal burdens have simply not been confined to minor regulatory offences.

In *R v Edwards*, Lawton LJ spoke of the need to construe the statute on which the charge was based to determine where the burden of proof lay. This task of interpretation was subsequently emphasised by the House of Lords in *R v Hunt* [1987], where it was held that the classification of defences for s 101 purposes was not constrained by the form of words used (eg 'to prove'), or their position in the statute creating the offence (eg whether it appeared as an exception or as a substantive element of the offence). A more subtle approach to interpretation was required, which would pay regard to the wording of the particular Act, but would also take into account the mischief at which it was aimed, as well as practical matters affecting the burden of proof. Some guidelines were suggested by Lord Griffiths:

- courts should be very slow to classify a defence as falling within s 101 (ie imposing a defence legal burden), because Parliament can never lightly be taken to have intended to impose an onerous duty on a defendant to prove his innocence in a criminal case;

- the ease and difficulty likely to be encountered by the parties in discharging a legal burden are of great importance;

- the gravity of the offence must be considered, as must the severity of the potential penalty.

But the task of interpretation is a difficult one, for at least four reasons:

- the question whether a given statutory provision falls within the class of 'any exception, exemption, proviso, excuse or qualification' is inherently problematic (see, for example, *Nimmo v Alexander Cowan and Sons Ltd* [1967]);

- s 101 has been haphazardly applied. Compare, for example, *Gatland v Metropolitan Police Commissioner* [1968] and *Nagy v Weston* [1965], and see offences under the Criminal Damage Act 1971;

- the project of distinguishing between rules and exceptions for s 101 purposes may be logically flawed because, rationally regarded, an exception is part of a rule;

- the reliance on policy that was authorised by *Nimmo v Alexander Cowan and Sons Ltd* [1967] and *R v Hunt* [1987] makes for uncertainty in interpretation.

▶ R v HUNT [1987]

Basic facts

Hunt was charged with possession of a controlled drug (morphine) contrary to s 5(2) of the Misuse of Drugs Act 1971. He had a compound mixture, which included morphine, but it was not unlawful to possess the compound provided that the morphine was less than 0.2% of the total and was not easily separated from the bulk. The prosecution failed to evidence the level of morphine, suggesting that this was for the defence to prove.

Relevance

The House of Lords construed the statute, concluding that the strength of the morphine was an essential ingredient of the offence, not an exception. And so the legal burden to prove strength lay with the prosecution.

Ordinarily then, the defence will have an evidential burden to establish any defence not subject to a specific legal burden, for example defences of self-defence (*R v Lobell* [1957]), duress (*R v Gill* [1963]), non-insane automatism (*Bratty v AG for Northern Ireland* [1963]) or provocation (*Mancini v DPP* [1942]). Note that the absence of consent in rape is an essential element of the offence, in respect of which the prosecution has both a legal and an evidential burden (*Selvey v DPP* [1970]).

REVERSE ONUS (LEGAL BURDENS) OF PROOF AND THE HUMAN RIGHTS ACT

It can be argued that imposing a legal burden of proof upon the accused may result in a violation of Article 6(2) (presumption of innocence). No such violation will occur if the imposition of a legal burden is reasonable and proportionate.

In the European Court of Human Rights case of *Salabiaku v France* [1988] the Court admitted that the presumption of innocence is not an absolute right, and held that a reverse onus is not in violation of Article 6, but must be kept within 'reasonable limits which take into account the importance of what is at stake and maintain the rights of the defence'.

REASONABLE AND PROPORTIONATE

Once it is suggested that a statutory provision imposes a legal burden on the defendant, the court will need to construe the statute and decide, using the factors identified in Hunt and subsequent cases, if a legal burden is indeed imposed and if that imposition is reasonable and proportionate. In construing the statute it is necessary to consider whether the statutory requirement requires the defendant 'to prove' the relevant fact in issue, how difficult it will be for the accused to prove the relevant fact in issue, the seriousness of the offence with which he is charged, the accused's rights, whether requiring the accused to prove the relevant fact in issue achieves a fair balance between the public interest and the protection of human rights for the individual, and Parliament's view concerning what is in the public interest (*R v DPP ex p Kebilene* [1994]).

If the Court does not believe that the imposition of a legal burden on the defendant would be reasonable and proportionate, the court may be required to read the provision down under s 3(1) of the Human Rights Act 1998 as merely imposing an evidential burden. This lowering of the burden for the defendant is often carried out in order to maintain the provision's compatibility with the Human Rights Act.

CASES IMPOSING AN EVIDENTIAL BURDEN

Reading a legal burden down to a mere evidential one was demonstrated in the case of *R v Lambert* [2001], which concerned a drug trafficking offence. Section 28(2) of the Misuse of Drugs Act 1971 provides a defence 'for the accused *to prove' lack* of knowledge of the presence of controlled drugs, which essentially provides that if the accused was not aware he was carrying drugs then he did not commit the offence. Where this defence is raised, it might be difficult for the prosecution to disprove it. The House of Lords, however, felt that requiring the accused to prove the defence (that he did not have knowledge) was disproportionate, given the possibility of a life sentence should the accused be unable to prove this defence to the requisite standard of proof (the balance of probabilities). Accordingly, in this case, the House of Lords held that the burden imposed upon the accused by the defence created by s 28(2) of the Misuse of Drugs Act 1971 should be read as imposing merely an evidential burden. [Note Lambert was decided before the Human Rights Act was in force, but in anticipation of it.]

> ### ▶ R v LAMBERT [2001]
>
> #### Basic facts
> This case involved possession of a Class A drug with intent to supply contrary to the Misuse of Drugs Act 1971. The case turned on section 5 of the Act and whether this reversed the legal burden of proof.
>
> #### Relevance
> As a result of this case, the legal burden of proof will not be placed on the defendant if it is disproportionate and the words in statutes, for example, 'prove', must be read down in a way compatible with the European Convention on Human Rights.

An interesting case is *Attorney-General's Reference (No 4 of 2002)* [2004]. Here the Terrorism Act 2000, which contains several provisions which explicitly place an evidential as opposed to a legal burden of proof on the defendant (note s 118(2)). But s 118(2) does not apply to all provisions of the Terrorism Act 2000 and therefore where it does not apply and the provision specifically stipulates 'for the defence to prove' is it safe to say that Parliament intended that particular provision to be a reverse onus? The defendant wished to use the defence included within s 11(2) to the offence of belonging to a proscribed organisation. According to s 11 of the Terrorism Act 2000:

'1   A person commits an offence if he belongs or professes to belong to a proscribed organisation.

2   It is a defence for a person charged with an offence under subsection (1) to prove—

(a) that the organisation was not proscribed on the last (or only) occasion on which he became a member or began to profess to be a member, and

(b) that he has not taken part in the activities of the organisation at any time while it was proscribed.'

By a 3 to 2 majority the House of Lords decided it should be read as imposing an evidential burden only. Lord Bingham for the majority considered s 11 to have been drawn very widely, covering persons who joined an organisation when it was not a terrorist organisation or when it was not proscribed, or as an immature juvenile.

Lord Bingham concluded that s 11(1) convictions could be on the basis of no blameworthy conduct. He also pointed out the difficulty of the defendant in evidencing the s 11(2) defence, since it might well be all but impossible for the defendant to show that he had not taken part in the activities of the organisation at any time while it was proscribed, particularly because such organisations do not generate minutes, records or documents on which he could rely. On this latter point, Lord Rodger for the minority suggested that the Crown would have similar difficulties in proving the defendant's affiliation. The minority view also focussed on the mischief of the statute, in that criminalising membership of terrorist organisations cut off vital resources, prohibited public demonstrations of support and reduced the credence of their purpose. For a s 11(1) offence the maximum penalty was ten year imprisonment. On balance, therefore, this was a serious crime with a potentially very serious penalty for what the majority of the House of Lords viewed as being a widely drawn offence. Ultimately, on this occasion these factors led to a reading of an evidential burden to ensure compatibility with Article 6.

CASES IMPOSING A LEGAL BURDEN

The decision in *Lambert* was thought to have opened the door to a great many legal burdens being read as merely evidential. Then the court took a slightly more robust approach in *R v Johnstone* [2003] 1 WLR 1736. Here, Lord Nicholls emphasised that it was parliament's role and not the court's to determine the constituent elements of a criminal offence and that such determination was based on a wide number of policy factors. The case concerned copyright infringement; the defendant was selling bootleg CDs. Again the penalty for the offence was potentially very serious: ten years' imprisonment. The defence open to the defendant was that he believed on reasonable grounds that use of the sign was not an infringement of the trade mark, in that either he was aware of the trade mark but did not believe his use infringed it, or was unaware of the existence of the trade mark. In this case, the House of Lords emphasised the strong public policy reasons for imposing the reverse onus, namely to combat counterfeiting and piracy, the awareness among traders of dealing in branded products, and the difficulty for prosecutors in proving dishonesty. On this occasion, this combination of factors led to the legal burden being upheld. In distinguishing when a legal burden will be upheld, some have suggested that *Lambert* remains the main authority in 'truly criminal offences' whereas *Johnstone* is authority for economic offences, but it is probably too much of a simplification.

In the second of the joined cases of *Attorney-General's Reference (No 4 of 2002)* and *Sheldrake v DPP* (conjoined appeals) [2005] 1 AC 264, the House of Lords in Sheldrake again upheld a legal burden. In *Sheldrake v DPP* at issue was the defence under s 5(2) of the Road Traffic Act 1988, which stipulates that when charged with being drunk in charge of a vehicle it is a defence 'to prove that at the time he is alleged to have committed the offence the circumstances were such that there was no likelihood of his driving the vehicle'. Again the wording of 'to prove' suggest a legal burden and the question for the court was whether it was reasonable and proportionate to impose one, or to read the burden to be merely an evidential one. The factors relied upon by the unanimous House of Lords in upholding the legal burden were that the offence had a legitimate purpose, being to prevent people from driving when drunk, and so protected other road users; the penalty was relatively minor (akin to a regulatory offence); it would be easier for the defendant to show what was on his mind 'as to make it much more appropriate for him to prove on the balance of probabilities that he would not have been likely to drive than for the prosecutor to prove, beyond reasonable doubt, that he would.'

▶ R (ON THE APPLICATION OF GRIFFIN) v RICHMOND MAGISTRATES' COURT [2008]

Basic facts
The defendant was charged with failing to hand over books and papers of the company to the liquidator contrary to s 208(1)(c) of the Insolvency Act 1986.

Relevance
The situation was held to be similar to that in Johnston, where the information was peculiarly within the defendant's knowledge and he will know what his motive was. The House of Lords upheld the legal burden.

A string of insolvency and bankruptcy cases have upheld legal burdens on the defendant, generally where the onus is on the defendant to prove that he had no intent to defraud (*Attorney-General's Reference (No 1 of 2004)* [2004]).

It is difficult to draw any firm conclusions from the case law, but it could be suggested that the legal burden is more likely to be read down to a mere evidential burden where the penalty is more serious and where it is perceived to be difficult for the defendant to prove the particular issue. Legal burdens would, therefore, be more likely to be upheld in the case of regulatory or minor offences which reflect a strong public policy. Economic offences or offences involving the carrying on of a trade needing specific knowledge, for example, or offences where the information is peculiarly within the defendant's own knowledge have been upheld as legal burdens (*R v Chargot Ltd (t/a Contract Services) and Others* [2008]). These aspects correlate with the notion that if a legal burden is imposed on the defendant and he is unable to prove that defence on the balance of probabilities he will be convicted. Imposing an evidential burden does not pose the same risk, but does still require the defendant to bring sufficient evidence to raise the issue and make it a live one.

THE PRIMA FACIE CASE

Before the defendant in a criminal trial will be called to provide a defence, the prosecution must have established a prima facie case (often termed a plea of 'no case to answer'). At the end of the Prosecution's case, therefore, the judge will need to decide (in the absence of the jury) whether the prosecution has made out a prima facie case; for which the prosecution will need to present at least some evidence in support of each of the 'facts in issue'. In *Jayasena v R* [1970] Lord Devlin described the requirement as

> such evidence as, if believed and left uncontradicted and un-explained, could be accepted by the jury as proof.

The decision is based on an assessment of the potential weight of the evidence, which in the Crown Court is whether the evidence is capable of proving the case beyond reasonable doubt (*R v Galbraith* [1981]).

In the Magistrates' court the decision is aided by the Practice Direction (Submission of No Case) [1962], which stipulates that the submission of no case to answer should succeed where, (1) there has been no evidence to prove an essential element of the offence charged, or (2) the prosecution evidence is so manifestly unreliable (or has been so discredited by cross-examination) that no reasonable tribunal could convict on it.

STANDARD OF PROOF

THE CRIMINAL STANDARD

Two formulae are traditional. Jurors may be told, 'You must be satisfied so that you are sure', or 'You must be satisfied beyond reasonable doubt' of the defendant's guilt. It is the effect of the summing up as a whole, however, that matters and the formulae do not have to be followed precisely, provided that their gist is explained to the jury (*R v Walters* [1969]).

Where there is a legal burden on the defendant to prove something in a criminal case, proof is required only to the civil standard of the balance of probabilities (*R v Carr-Briant* [1943]).

THE CIVIL STANDARD

A lower standard of proof is required in civil cases: proof on the balance of probabilities, often written in the mathematical formulation of 51% (*Miller v Minister of Pensions* [1947]). Where a serious allegation is made, for example, of conduct amounting to a criminal offence, proof is still only to the civil standard. The inherent improbability of such an allegation is taken into account when deciding whether the evidence is of sufficient weight to satisfy the court that the allegation has been proved. Earlier suggestions that a third standard existed, at some point between the ordinary civil standard and the criminal standard, were discredited in *Re H* [1996] by the House of Lords.

PRESUMPTIONS OF FACT AND LAW

There are three types of presumption:

1   presumptions of fact;
2   irrebuttable presumptions of law;
3   rebuttable presumptions of law.

PRESUMPTIONS OF FACT

A 'presumption of fact' is no more than an inference from facts that is part of the ordinary reasoning process. For example, by s 8 of the Criminal Justice Act 1967, there is a presumption of fact that people intend the natural consequences of their acts. The section provides that a court or jury, in determining whether a person has committed an offence, shall not be *bound in law* to infer that he intended the result of his actions by reason of its being a natural and probable consequence of those actions, but shall decide whether he did intend that result *by drawing inferences from all the evidence*.

IRREBUTTABLE PRESUMPTIONS OF LAW

These are just the same as rules or principles of substantive law. For example, 'the presumption of innocence' is a way of referring to the principle that the burden of proof generally rests on the prosecution in a criminal case.

REBUTTABLE PRESUMPTIONS OF LAW

The general pattern of these presumptions is that, once a party has proved certain basic facts, other facts will be presumed to exist, in the absence of some evidence to the contrary. The amount of contrary evidence required depends on the substantive law applying to the particular situation.

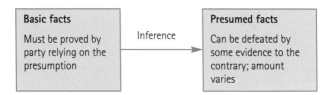

Basic facts

Must be proved by party relying on the presumption

Inference

Presumed facts

Can be defeated by some evidence to the contrary; amount varies

PRESUMPTION OF MARRIAGE

Where the couple have gone through a ceremony of marriage (and presumably now a civil partnership) followed by cohabitation, there is a presumption that the ceremony was valid. The presumption can be rebutted by evidence to the contrary on the balance of probabilities (*Re H* [1996]). Even where there is no evidence that a ceremony of marriage has been performed, a presumption that a man and woman were lawfully married will arise from evidence of cohabitation, coupled with their reputation as man and wife (*Re Taylor (Dec'd)* [1961]).

PRESUMPTION OF LEGITIMACY

There is a presumption that a child born or conceived during wedlock is the child of the woman's husband. By s 26 of the Family Law Reform Act 1969, the presumption may be rebutted by evidence that shows that it is more probable than not that the person in question is legitimate or illegitimate, as the case may be.

PRESUMPTION OF DEATH

Some statutory provisions require a court to presume the death of a person in certain circumstances. There is also a common law presumption of death, as follows:

Where as regards a certain person there is no acceptable evidence that he was alive at some time during a continuous period of seven years or more, then he will be presumed to have died at some time during that period if it can be proved that:

- there are persons who would be likely to have heard of him during that period;
- those persons have not heard of him; and
- all due inquiries have been made appropriate to the circumstances.

Res ipsa loquitur

This maxim, meaning 'the thing speaks for itself', was traditionally regarded as giving rise to some kind of presumption in actions for negligence. Where something which had caused an accident was shown to have been under the management of the defendant or his servants, and the accident was such that in the ordinary course of things did not happen if those who had management used proper care, the accident itself led to an inference of negligence (*George v Eagle Air Services Ltd and Others* [2009], involving an air crash in which the court rejected the notion that aeroplane crashes happen in the absence of fault and held that it was, 'not unreasonable to place on the [operators] the burden of producing an explanation which was at least consistent with absence of fault on their part').

PRESUMPTION OF REGULARITY

This expression can refer to two different presumptions:

- the presumption that official appointments have been properly and formally made, and that official acts have been properly and formally performed (*R v Verelst* [1813]);

- the presumption that a mechanical instrument, provided it is of a kind that is usually in working order, was in working order at a particular time that is relevant in the litigation. The presumption has been said to apply to watches and speedometers (*Nicholas v Penney* [1950]), to traffic lights (*Tingle Jacobs and Co v Kennedy* [1964]), and now computers (see Sched 2 to the Civil Evidence Act 1995; s 60 of the Youth Justice and Criminal Evidence Act 1999).

PRESUMPTION AND THE EUROPEAN CONVENTION ON HUMAN RIGHTS

Where a presumption operates against the defendant in the context of criminal proceedings, this will not necessarily give rise to a violation of Article 6(2) (presumption of innocence). Whether there has been a breach of Article 6(2) will again depend on whether the presumption lies within reasonable limits (*R v DPP ex p Kebilene* [1994]). In determining this, the court will consider the same factors as outlined above for imposing a legal burden.

FACTS NOT REQUIRING PROOF

The general rule is that, if a party wants to rely on a particular fact in support of his case, that fact must be formally proved by providing evidence of it at trial. To this rule there are two important exceptions:

- formal admissions; and
- judicial notice.

FORMAL ADMISSIONS

CIVIL TRIALS

By r 14.1 of the Civil Procedure Rules 1998 (CPR), a party may admit the truth of the whole or any part of another party's case. He may do this by giving notice in writing, for example, in a statement of case or by letter.

A notice to admit facts may be served under r 32.18 of the CPR. Such a notice must be served no later than 21 days before the trial. Where the other party makes any admission in response to the notice, the admission may be used against him only:

- in the proceedings in which the notice is served; and
- by the party who served the notice.

CRIMINAL TRIALS

By s 10(1) of the Criminal Justice Act 1967:

- any fact of which oral evidence may be given in any criminal proceedings may be admitted for the purpose of those proceedings by or on behalf of the prosecutor or defendant;

■ the admission of any such fact shall, as against the party making the admission, be conclusive evidence in those proceedings of the fact admitted.

By s 10(2), an admission under s 10(1) may be made before or at the proceedings, but, if made otherwise than in court, it must be in writing.

By s 10(3), an admission under this section for the purpose of proceedings relating to any matter shall be treated as an admission for the purpose of any subsequent criminal proceedings relating to that matter (including any appeal or retrial).

By s 10(4), an admission under this section may with the leave of the court be withdrawn in the proceedings for the purpose of which it is made or any subsequent criminal proceedings relating to the same matter.

A Practice Direction of 1995 provides that where there is a plea of not guilty at a plea and directions hearing, both prosecution and defence are expected to inform the court of facts which are to be admitted and which can be reduced into writing under s 10(2).

JUDICIAL NOTICE

'Judicial notice' refers to the acceptance by a judicial tribunal of the truth of a fact without formal proof, on the ground that it is within the knowledge of the tribunal itself. There are three types:

■ Facts Judicially Noticed 'Without Inquiry': facts accepted from the judge's general knowledge of them as being regarded as matters of common knowledge; examples include, clearing banks in the UK usually charge compound, rather than simple, interest (*Bello v Barclays Bank plc* [1994]); temperatures fall at night (*Watts v Reigate and Banstead BC* [1984]).

■ Facts Judicially Noticed 'After Inquiry': facts accepted from inquiries made by the judge for his own information from sources to which it is proper for him to refer, including a dictionary, certificates from responsible officials, letters from Secretaries of State or statements made in court by counsel on their behalf, works of reference and the oral statements of witnesses;

examples include, where information is required about current political or diplomatic matters namely whether a person was entitled to diplomatic immunity (*Engelke v Musman* [1928]); where information is required about historical facts such as there was currently a very turbulent political situation in Hebron (*Re A-R* [1997]); and where information is required about customs, including professional practices, such as the practice of the Comptroller General's Office in relation to applications for patents (*Alliance Flooring Co Ltd v Winsorflor Ltd* [1961]).

■ Statutory Provisions: several Acts of Parliament direct the courts to take judicial notice of various matters, for example, by s 3(2) of the European Communities Act 1972, judicial notice is to be taken of various treaties, of the Official Journal of the Communities and of any decision of, or expression of opinion by, the European Court on questions concerning the meaning or effect of any of the treaties or Community instruments.

USE OF PERSONAL KNOWLEDGE

While it seems clear that a tribunal may make use of its *general* knowledge by virtue of judicial notice, it is also said that neither judges nor jurors can make use of their purely personal knowledge in reaching a decision.

But the Divisional Court has, on several occasions, held that *magistrates* have properly applied their own knowledge of local conditions (*Ingram v Percival* [1969]; *Paul v DPP* [1990]).

In *Wetherall v Harrison* [1976], the Divisional Court emphasised that, although such special knowledge could be used to *interpret* the evidence given in court, it must not be used to *contradict* it. In *Bowman v DPP* [1990], it was said that justices must be extremely circumspect in using their own local knowledge. They should inform the parties if they are likely to use such knowledge, so as to give an opportunity for comment on the knowledge that they claim to have.

You should now be confident that you would be able to tick all of the boxes on the checklist at the beginning of this chapter. To check your knowledge of Burden of proof why not visit the companion website and take the Multiple Choice Question test. Check your understanding of the terms and vocabulary used in this chapter with the flashcard glossary.

3

Unfair and illegally obtained evidence

JUDICIAL DISCRETION TO EXCLUDE EVIDENCE

Civil Cases

Under the Civil Procedure Rules the Court has the power to control the case and the evidence presented in it, consequently the Court can exclude evidence. Rule 32.1(2) stipulates, 'The court may use its power under this rule to exclude evidence that would otherwise be admissible.'

▶ JONES v UNIVERSITY OF WARWICK [2003]

Basic facts

The claimant injured her hand at work and claimed significant continuing disability. Secret filming of the claimant at home made by a private investigator (posing as a market researcher) for the employer's insurer showed otherwise.

Relevance

The court recognised two conflicting public interests: the court emphasised the benefit to the court of having this relevant evidence, but admonished the tactics of trespass and breach of Article 8 of the European Convention on Human Rights. These are factors to weigh in the balance when undertaking its management or proceedings role and doing justice between the parties. The court required the insurers to pay the costs of litigation.

Criminal Cases

In criminal cases the judge has discretion to exclude otherwise relevant evidence under s 78 of the Police and Criminal Evidence Act 1984 (PACE) and under the common law (s 82(3) of PACE preserves the discretion at common law but this has been largely superseded by the statutory discretion in practice). Generally, evidence will be excluded if it was obtained by illegal means or on the basis of fairness. This was not always the position, note the decision in *R v Sang* [1980] regarding evidence obtained illegally, which was specifically reversed in PACE 1984.

> **R v SANG [1980]**

Basic facts

An undercover police officer posed as a buyer of forged currency to Sang. Sang had previous convictions for forgery. Sang pleaded 'entrapment', while not a defence, he sought the judge's discretion to exclude the evidence on the basis of ensuring a fair trial.

Relevance

Under the common law position in 1980 the Court reasoned that only the reliability of the evidence mattered, not how the evidence was obtained.

THE COMMON LAW DISCRETION TO EXCLUDE

The common law discretion to exclude otherwise relevant evidence is not limited only to illegally and unfairly obtained evidence. *Sang* confirmed the discretion to exclude evidence on the basis that its prejudicial effect outweighed its probative value (essentially that the evidence would engender too much prejudicial effect in the mind of jury for it to be used, for example showing the jury gruesome photographs of how a child had been killed). The effect of s 82(3) of PACE is to retain the common law discretion. The common law discretion was valuable in *R v Sat-Bhambra* [1989] where serious doubt had been cast on the reliability of the evidence admitted (here a confession) but the court held that s 76, and s 78, could not apply to exclude evidence that had already been admitted. The court instead used the preserved common law discretion to exclude the evidence.

Please also refer to Chapter 8 on the exclusion of confession evidence.

EVIDENCE OBTAINED BY ILLEGAL OR UNFAIR MEANS

According to s 78 PACE:

1   In any proceeding the court may refuse to allow evidence on which the prosecution proposes to rely to be given if it appears to the court that, having regard to all the circumstances, including the circumstances in

which the evidence was obtained, the admission of the evidence would have *such an adverse effect on the fairness of the proceedings* that the court ought not to admit it.

2   Nothing in this section shall prejudice *any rule of law requiring a court to exclude evidence.*

The following points of interpretation should be noted:

▓ the exclusionary discretion only applies to prosecution evidence;

▓ the exclusionary discretion applies to all prosecution evidence, even if that particular type of evidence is covered by another specific provision (such as s 76 PACE on confessions, *R v Mason* [1988], and s 101 of the Criminal Justice Act 2003 on bad character evidence, *R v Weir and Others* [2005]);

▓ the evidence must be evidence on which the prosecution *proposes* to rely; it is too late to use the sub-section if the evidence has already been given (*R v Sat-Bhambra* [1989]);

▓ it is not enough that the admission of the evidence will have *some* adverse effect; the adverse effect must be so great that the court ought not to admit the evidence (*R v Walsh* [1990]). Once that stage has been reached, however, the judge must exclude the evidence – despite the use of 'may' in the opening words of the sub-section (*R v Chalkley* [1998]);

▓ the 'fairness of the proceedings' has been defined to refer only to that part of the proceedings taking place at trial (*R v Mason* [1988]). Some suggest that this interpretation is inconsistent with the specific wording chosen by Parliament;

▓ it is fairness of the proceedings that the judge has to consider. Fairness to the defendant is part of this idea, but so is fairness to the prosecution (*R v Robb* [1991]);

▓ the inclusion within s 78 of the phrase 'including the circumstances in which the evidence was obtained' effectively reverses the previous position at common law in *Sang* as far as the statutory discretion is concerned. Consequently, the way in which the evidence is obtained can be reason for its exclusion if its admission would have such an adverse effect on the fairness of the proceedings. Evidence obtained illegally will not always be excluded; the judge must apply the exclusionary test in the normal way.

The discretion is often at issue where evidence has allegedly been obtained by unlawful or unfair means such as:

- police entrapment

- improper or unlawful means to gain evidence (including unlawful seizure), including trickery

- unauthorised surveillance

- breach of PACE provisions or the Codes of Conduct (especially police bad faith)

- evidence from unlawfully obtained samples.

THE EXERCISE OF THE DISCRETION

The Court of Appeal has given trial judges a very free hand in their operation of s 78(1) and has subjected their decisions to a minimum of review. In *R v Samuel* [1988], the Court of Appeal said that it was undesirable to attempt any general guidance as to the way in which a judge's discretion under s 78 should be exercised and in *R v Jelen* [1989] and *R v Roberts* [1997] the Court of Appeal made the same point, saying that this was not an apt field for hard case law and well founded distinctions between cases.

R v Loosley [2001] suggests s 78 (in the context other than confessions and evidence obtained after the commission of the offence) is directed *primarily* with whether the impropriety affected the reliability of the evidence obtained or undermined his ability to challenge the evidence to the extent that the fairness of the trial is affected. Its purpose is not, therefore, to discipline the police for impropriety, that is the role of the abuse of process doctrine (below), but the courts have on occasion admonished police behaviour and trickery. In practice, the two mechanisms are very similar and do overlap; the defendant could try to get the whole case thrown out as an abuse of process or if unsuccessful try to have the evidence obtained as a result of police impropriety excluded.

Several cases show that the Court of Appeal will interfere with a trial judge's exercise of his discretion under s 78(1) only for '*Wednesbury* unreasonableness' (see, for example, *R v Christou* [1992]; *R v McEvoy* [1997]).

There is no burden of proof for s 78 discretion; it is the decision of the trial judge, and therefore unlike s 76 PACE which requires the party adducing the confession to prove it was not obtained in circumstances affecting its reliability or by oppression (*R (Saifi) v Governor of Brixton Prison and another* [2001]).

In addition to a breach of PACE, any other domestic law, a foreign law or Articles of the European Convention on Human Rights, a breach of one of the Codes of Practice may cause the evidence to be excluded under s 78(1). As the Court of Appeal said in *R v Elson* [1994], the Codes exist to protect the individual against the might of the State. The court added that the individual is at a great disadvantage when arrested by the police, and this is so whether or not the police have behaved with the utmost propriety. Breach of the Codes, however, will not lead to automatic exclusion of evidence (*R v Keenan* [1989]; *R v Kelly* [1998]).

In *Attorney-General's Reference (No 3 of 1999)* [2001] the defendant objected to the use of evidence obtained due to the unlawful retention of a DNA sample which should have been destroyed following the defendant's acquittal (s 64(3B) PACE now repealed). The House of Lords held that it was not mandatory to exclude evidence obtained due to an unlawful retention of a DNA sample under s 64(3B) PACE, but left the question to the discretion of the trial judge under s 78. Controversially, amendments to PACE then allowed the blanket retention of DNA evidence and fingerprints of all arrested persons, whether convicted or not. In *S and Marper v United Kingdom* [2008] the Grand Chamber of the European Court of Human Rights found the UK's blanket retention policies in breach of Article 8; but does this address the question of whether, if unlawfully retained, such samples can be used in evidence?

In short, not every breach of PACE, other legal provisions or the Codes of Practice will result in the exclusion of evidence obtained due to that breach under s 78 (*R v P* [2002]). Certainly the European Court of Human Rights has directed that any use of evidence obtained by torture would be automatically excluded, but has left open the issue regarding breaches of 'inhuman or degrading treatment' (*A v Secretary of State for the Home Department (No 2)* [2005]; *Jalloh v Germany* [2007]). Some Code provisions, however, are relatively minor and therefore to exclude evidence on that basis might often lead to disproportionality. Exclusion is not automatic. Whether the judge exercises discretion to exclude the evidence will turn on the particular circumstances of the case.

Where the issue is illegally obtained evidence case law suggests that it is likely to be excluded under the discretion only if the breach is 'significant and substantial' (*R v Keenan* [1990]). Important safeguards for the defendant/suspect were included within PACE, such as the right of access to legal representation under s 58 and the need for the police to make contemporaneous notes of interviews. Breaches of the more significant provisions such as these could be classified as 'significant and substantial' so as to lead to the exclusion of any confession or other evidence produced as a result of the breach. In *R v Parris* [1988] the defendant's confession was excluded because the Court was of the view that had a solicitor been present the accused would have accepted his advice to remain silent.

▶ R v KEENAN [1990]

Basic facts
The defendant was charged with taking a vehicle without consent and possession of an offensive weapon (a spear). A contemporaneous record of the defendant's statement was not made. This was a breach of Code of Practice C.

Relevance
These provisions were intended to provide safeguards against the police inaccurately recording or inventing the words used in questioning a detained person and to make it difficult for a detained person to make unfounded allegations that the police had inaccurately recorded or invented an interview. Where there had been significant and substantial breaches of those provisions by the police the evidence so obtained ought to be excluded.

Violation of fundamental provisions, such as the right of access to legal advice, will not always lead to the exercise of the discretion to exclude evidence obtained as a result. For example in *R v Alladice* [1988] the Court was of the opinion that because the defendant was aware of his legal rights and was able to cope with the interview, and had also exercised his then right to remain silent, the breach of s 58 in this case did not 'have such an adverse effect on the fairness of the proceedings' that the court ought not to admit the confession. Every serious breach of PACE, therefore, will not guarantee exclusion of the evidence obtained.

The judge will assess the affect of the breach, and any subsequent evidence elicited due to that breach, on the fairness of the proceedings. If the police act in bad faith that assessment is a little easier to make, the Court will usually hold a bad faith breach to have affected the fairness of the proceedings. Otherwise, as in *Alladice* the test is 'if the rest of the evidence was strong, excluding the improperly obtained evidence would not affect the result of the trial, whereas if the rest of the evidence was weak the protection of the rules was most needed.'

Unfairly obtained evidence includes evidence obtained by a trick or deceit played on the defendant by the police in order to induce him to confess or to incriminate himself. But again not all police ruses or tricks will lead to the exclusion of the evidence obtained; cases will always turn on their own facts. In *R v Mason* [1988] the defendant was informed by the police, untruthfully, that his fingerprint had been identified at the crime scene. The defendant's solicitor advised him to confess, which he duly did. The Court viewed this trick as being particularly serious as not only was it played on the defendant but was also played on his solicitor who must know the truth in order to advise his client properly. The evidence obtained was thus excluded.

SECTION 78 AND ENTRAPMENT

Undercover operations raise particular issues for the notion of exclusion of unfairly and illegally obtained evidence, especially where the evidence secured is clearly reliable. Police entrapment is not a defence. The key issue with evidence obtained by entrapment (or the use of *agents provocateurs*) is whether the undercover police officer is merely setting up an opportunity for a person to commit a crime (*Williams v DPP* [1993]) or is pressuring someone to commit a crime that they would otherwise not commit.

▶ WILLLIAMS v DPP [1993]

Basic facts

Undercover police officers had left an unattended van full of (dummy) cigarette cartons. The defendant attempted to steal them.

Relevance

The Court held, 'the police had done nothing to force, persuade, encourage or coerce the appellants and therefore had not acted as *agents provocateurs* by participating in, procuring or counselling the commission of any crime. The appellants had voluntarily taken the goods in the absence of any pressure from the police and with full understanding of their dishonesty.'

In *R v Smurthwaite* [1994], the Court of Appeal listed some of the factors to be regarded when considering the admissibility of evidence obtained during an undercover operation:

- Was the officer acting as an *agent provocateur* in the sense that he was enticing a defendant to commit an offence he would not otherwise have committed?

- What was the nature of the entrapment?

- Does the evidence consist of admissions to a completed offence, or does it consist of the actual commission of an offence?

- How active or passive was the officer's role in obtaining the evidence?

- Is there an unassailable record of what occurred, or is there strong supporting evidence?

- Did the officer abuse his undercover role to ask questions which ought properly to have been asked as a police officer and in accordance with the Codes?

Cases in which undercover police officers have posed as buyers or decoys tend not to have resulted in evidence being excluded if the officers behaved as a normal customer in that situation (*Nottingham City Council v Amin* [2000] taxi driven in area not covered by its licence). If the officers instead instigate or encourage the commission of an offence which the defendant would not ordinarily commit this may lead to the exclusion of the evidence, or a stay of the proceedings as an abuse of process (*Attorney-General's Reference (No 3 of 2000)* [2001]). Authorisation for such operations is also an important factor; lack of authorisation will more likely lead to exclusion of evidence.

ABUSE OF PROCESS

As part of the inherent jurisdiction of the courts (in civil and criminal cases) a case can be stayed for abuse of process. In relation to illegal, unfair or improper police conduct, rather than rely on s 78 the court may, where appropriate, stay the proceedings as an abuse of process (*R v Latif* [1996]). Where the case is stayed as an abuse of process (essentially an abuse of the power of state agents) the case will not be tried at all on the basis that it is an affront to the principles of justice and fairness (*Teixeira de Castro v Portugal* [1988]). The purpose of the doctrine is to uphold the integrity of the criminal justice system and deter state agents from abusing their power. The pivotal case on abuse of process and entrapment is the joined cases of *R v Loosely* and *Attorney-General's Reference (No 3 of 2000)* [2001].

> ### ▶ R v LOOSELY AND ATTORNEY-GENERAL'S REFERENCE (No 3 of 2000) [2001]
>
> #### Basic facts
>
> In Loosely, having learned the name of a drugs supplier in a bar, the undercover officer purchased heroin from L. In AG Reference the defendant sold contraband cigarettes to undercover officers, but was also persuaded to arrange a supply of heroin.
>
> #### Relevance
>
> The House of Lords found that while in Loosely the officers had not incited a crime that L would otherwise not commit, since he was a supplier of Class A drugs, in AG Reference the defendant told the officers that heroin was not his trade but felt obliged to return favours following when the officers presented cigarettes as inducements. Thus in AG Reference the case was rightly stayed.

The reference to the House of Lords in *AG Reference* was whether Article 6 European Convention on Human Rights had modified either the s 78 discretion or abuse of process doctrine. The House held that it had not.

In *R v Shannon* [2001] it was recognised that the abuse of process doctrine may be used where the impropriety is that of a state agent, not a private citizen such as a newspaper reporter. In *A v Secretary of State for the Home Depart-*

ment (No 2) [2005] considering the admissibility of statements made under torture abroad (thus not induced by British state agents) the House of Lords stated that to admit such evidence would be 'incompatible with the principles which should animate a tribunal seeking to administer justice'.

INTERCEPT EVIDENCE

Section 17 of the Regulation of Investigatory Powers Act 2000 prohibits the admission of evidence which discloses 'any of the contents of an intercepted communication'. This is a public policy decision to protect the security services and their methods of crime detection.

Bugging of telephones and buildings, for example, that do not involve the interception of a transmission would appear to fall under the normal rules of s 78 discretion to exclude (*Khan v United Kingdom* [2000] regarding covert bugging of premises).

You should now be confident that you would be able to tick all of the boxes on the checklist at the beginning of this chapter. To check your knowledge of Unfair and illegally obtained evidence why not visit the companion website and take the Multiple Choice Question test. Check your understanding of the terms and vocabulary used in this chapter with the flashcard glossary.

4

Competence, compellability and special measures directions

Competence refers to a person having the legal ability to give evidence. Compellability refers to the issue of being *compelled* or *forced* by law to give evidence, and is enforced by 'contempt of court' proceedings. In order to enhance the testimony of more vulnerable witnesses the court will, in certain circumstances, allow for evidence to be given by special means, such as live link or pre-recorded. The topic of competence also includes the notion of sworn and unsworn evidence.

CIVIL CASES

In civil proceedings the parties to the proceedings are competent to give evidence and can compel others to give evidence, including the spouses of parties (s 1 of the Evidence Amendment Act 1853). Witness statements may be exchanged and serve as the evidence-in-chief of those witnesses. The court may allow any witness to give evidence by means of a video link or other means (Rule 32.3 Civil Procedure Rules 1998).

There are special rules for children, defined as under 18 years of age (s 105 Children Act 1989).

CHILDREN IN CIVIL CASES

A child may give sworn evidence if he can satisfy the test in *R v Hayes* [1977], such that he understands:

- the solemnity of the occasion; and

- the special duty to tell the truth, over and above the ordinary social duty to do so.

If the child does not satisfy these conditions, he may be able to give evidence under s 96 of the Children Act 1989. By this section, a child who does not understand the nature of an oath may give unsworn evidence if:

- he understands that it is his duty to speak the truth; and

- he has sufficient understanding to justify his evidence being heard.

PERSONS OF IMPAIRED INTELLECT IN CIVIL CASES

Competence depends on the nature and severity of the disability, which may be investigated in open court before testimony is received. The test to be applied is whether, despite any mental disability, the witness understands the nature of the oath in the light of the *Hayes* test (*R v Bellamy* [1985]).

CRIMINAL CASES

The basic rebuttable rule is that all persons are competent and compellable to give evidence in criminal proceedings (s 53 Youth Justice and Criminal Evidence Act 1999 (YJCEA)).

By sub-s (3), a person is not competent to give evidence if it appears to the court that he is not a person who is able to:

(a) understand questions put to him as a witness; and

(b) give answers to it which can be understood.

Any question whether a witness in criminal proceedings is competent may be raised by either a party to the proceedings or by the court of its own motion (ie, by the judge, even if none of the parties raises the issue). It is plainly advisable to take any objection to competency before the witness is sworn or starts to give evidence, although it may only arise as an issue during cross-examination if the witness gave video-recorded evidence-in-chief (*R v Powell* [2006]). If such a question arises, the procedure set out in s 54 will be followed. Available special measures directions must also be taken into account when the court is determining competence (s 54(3) YJCEA for criminal cases).

It is for the party calling the witness to satisfy the court that, *on a balance of probabilities*, the witness is competent (s 54(2)). It should be noted that this civil standard applies to both the defence and prosecution. The issue must be determined in the absence of the jury, if there is one (s 54(4)). Expert evidence may be received on the question (s 54(5)). Any questioning of the witness, where the court considers that necessary, shall be conducted by the court in the presence of the parties (s 54(6)). In other words, the potential witness will not be submitted to examination and cross-examination by counsel, but may be questioned by the judge.

Competency to give evidence

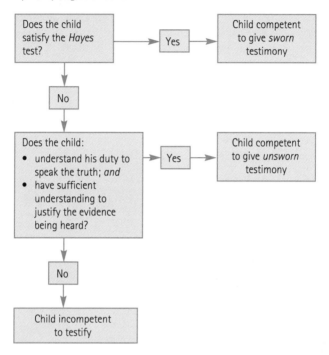

In *R v MacPherson* [2006] it was said that the test of competence in s 53(3) is one of understanding and there was no requirement that the witness should be aware of his status as a witness. The court added that questions as to reliability and credibility went to weight, not competence.

▶ R v SED [2005]

Basic facts

The witness in an alleged attempted rape suffered from Alzheimer's disease, causing a loss of memory and confusion.

Relevance

The court held that competence does not always require 100%, or near 100%, mutual understanding between questioner and questioned. It is thus for the judge to determine the question of competence almost as a matter of feel, taking into account the effect of the potential witness' performance as a whole, whether there is a common and comprehensible thread in his or her responses to the questions, however patchy – bearing always in mind that, if, on critical matters, the witness can be seen and heard to be intelligible, it is for the jury and no-one else to determine matters of reliability and general cogency.

There are special rules for four types of witnesses:

- Defendants
- The defendant's spouse or civil partner
- Children
- Persons of impaired intellect.

DEFENDANTS IN CRIMINAL CASES

All defendants are competent, but not compellable, witnesses in their own defence, or in the defence of a co-accused (s 1(1) of the Criminal Evidence Act 1898).

An accused person is incompetent as a witness for the prosecution (s 53(4) of the Youth Justice and Criminal Evidence Act 1999). Where two or more persons are charged and the prosecution wishes to use the evidence of one against the other(s), it is necessary to separate that person from his companions so that he ceases to be their co-accused (s 53(5) YJCEA). This will usually be done by:

- discontinuing proceedings against the potential witness;
- obtaining a plea of guilty from the potential witness before trial of his companions.

Where a defendant gives evidence at his own trial, he must do so on oath or affirmation and will be liable to cross-examination (s 1(2) Criminal Evidence Act 1898). His testimony will be evidence at the trial *for all purposes*. Thus, he may incriminate himself in the witness box, and anything he says there may be used as evidence against any co-defendant (*R v Rudd* [1948]). Counsel for the prosecution is entitled to cross-examine with a view to incriminating him or any co-defendant (*R v Paul* [1920]). He may also be cross-examined on behalf of any co-defendant.

If a defendant fails to give evidence in his own defence (or, when giving evidence, refuses without good cause to answer any question), the court or jury, in determining whether he is guilty of the offence charged, may draw adverse inferences from that failure as appear proper (s 35 of the Criminal Justice and Public Order Act 1994). For this provision to apply, the prosecution must first have made out a prima facie case on the basis of their own evidence, and the defendant must:

■ have pleaded not guilty (s 35(1));

■ be physically and mentally fit to testify (s 35(1));

■ be aware of the risks attached to silence (s 35(2)).

Where the judge rules that it would not be undesirable for the accused to testify despite suffering from a physical or mental condition, the jury should be made aware of the condition. In this way the jury can take it into account in reaching a fair assessment of the defendant's evidence (*R v Anwoir* [2008]).

▶ R v FRIEND (No 2) [2004]

Basic facts

In *Friend* [1997] the defendant had a mental age of 9 (actually aged 15). Inferences were drawn from his silence and he was convicted. On a referral to the Criminal Cases Review Committee the Court of Appeal took fresh evidence that he had attention deficit and hyperactivity disorder (ADHD) which means that he would have been easily distracted and inconsistent.

Relevance

The court held that the nature and extent of the defendant's problems were not fully appreciated at trial, and so held the conviction to be unsafe. In *Friend* [1997] the court referred to examples of conditions under s 35(1)(b), 'risk of an epileptic attack, latent schizophrenia where the experience of giving evidence might trigger a florid state.' *Friend (No 2)* broadens the examples of conditions that might avoid adverse inferences from silence to include ADHD.

If the case is one where a jury would be entitled to draw an inference under s 35, the judge must direct them in his summing up that:

- the burden of proof remains on the prosecution;

- the defendant is entitled not to give evidence;

- the jury must be satisfied there is a case to answer before drawing any inferences from silence;

- the jury cannot convict solely on an inference drawn from silence;

- no inference is to be drawn unless the jury are sure that there is no other reasonable explanation, consistent with innocence, to account for the defendant's silence.

(See *R v Cowan* [1997]; *R v Friend* [1997]; *R v Friend (No 2)* [2004] and *R v Kavanagh* [2005]).

Similarly, a defendant in a civil case who chooses not to testify runs the risk that his silence, in circumstances where he would be expected to answer, might convert slight evidence against him into proof (*Gibbs v Rea* [1998]).

▶ R v COWAN [1997]

Basic facts
This case involved an appeal against the defendant's convictions for unlawful wounding, doing an act tending and intended to pervert the course of public justice and attempted theft. The first argument was that s 35 should apply only in exceptional cases. This was because it infringed the defendant's right of silence, and altered the burden of proof by putting the burden on the defendant to testify in order to avoid conviction. The second argument was that the trial judge's directions when applying s 35 were wrong.

Relevance

Allowing the appeal the Court of Appeal presented the court with a list of essential issues which should be contained in a direction to the jury in future cases (above). In addition s 35 should not be limited to exceptional circumstances. The right to silence was expressly preserved. The prosecution still had to establish a prima facie case first and the defendant could not be convicted on a s 35 adverse inference alone. The standard of proof also remained the same.

SPOUSES AND CIVIL PARTNERS OF DEFENDANTS IN CRIMINAL CASES

Section 53(1) of the YJCEA provides that, at every stage in criminal proceedings, all persons are (whatever their age) *competent* to give evidence. It follows that a defendants's husband or wife (spouse) or civil partner is always competent for the prosecution. The only possible exceptions to this would occur where the spouse/civil partner failed to satisfy the requirements for competence contained in s 53(3), or where he or she was a defendant in the same proceedings. In that case, the spouse would be incompetent for the prosecution by virtue of s 53(4). It follows from the very wide terms of s 53(1) of the YJCEA that a defendant's spouse/civil partner will also be competent for the defendant and for any co-accused.

By s 80(2) of the Police and Criminal Evidence Act 1984 (PACE), the defendant's spouse/civil partner is always compellable as a witness for the defendant. But this provision is again subject to s 80(4), which provides that no person who is charged in any proceedings shall be compellable under s 80 to give evidence in those proceedings. So, if a husband and wife or civil partners are both charged in the same proceedings, the husband, for example, cannot compel the wife under s 80(2) to give evidence for him and she cannot compel him to give evidence for her.

The defendant's spouse will, again subject to sub-s (4), be compellable for the prosecution and for her spouse's/civil partner's co-accused, but only in relation to offences that are 'specified' (s 80(2A)). In other words, the defendant's spouse/civil partner is compellable for a co-accused only in those circumstances where he or she would be compellable for the prosecution. The reason for this is that, since the prosecution cannot compel the spouse/civil partner to give evidence in trials for offences that are not 'specified', it would be wrong for someone jointly charged with the defendant to be able to do so because the result would be to give the prosecution an indirect advantage through the opportunity for cross-examination. For example, if the husband and a co-accused are charged with handling stolen goods, the wife would not be a compellable witness for the prosecution because handling stolen goods is not a 'specified' offence. But, if the co-accused could compel the wife to give evidence in his defence, she could be cross-examined by the prosecution and during the course of that cross-examination she might have to provide answers that would support the case against her husband.

The 'specified' offences are set out in s 80(3) of PACE. They are offences where:

(a) the offence charged involves an assault on, or injury or a threat of injury to, the spouse/civil partner of the defendant or a person who was at the material time under the age of 16;

(b) the offence charged is a sexual offence alleged to have been committed in respect of a person who was at the material time under the age of 16;

(c) the offence charged consists of attempting or conspiring to commit either of the above, or being a secondary party to or inciting either of the above.

There is at least one problem with the interpretation of these provisions. It concerns what is referred to in sub-s (3)(a) as an offence that 'involves an assault on, or injury or a threat of injury to' the spouse/civil partner of the defendant or a person who was at the material time under the age of 16. The sub-section clearly covers an offence such as robbery where violence, or the threat of it, is an essential element of the offence. But it is unclear whether 'involves' covers an offence where this is not the case and the violence is only an incidental element. In *R v McAndrew-Bingham* [1998], the same wording in s 32(2)(a) of the Criminal Justice Act 1988 was given the broader interpretation, but this was in the context of a provision for the use of video and live link TV wherever a child witness was likely to be traumatised by confrontation with the defendant. The court adopted a purposive construction, but it is by no means clear that a purposive construction of s 80(3) of PACE would have the same result.

The choice of a spouse or civil partner to give evidence (where s/he is not compellable), exists right up to the moment s/he enters the witness box, and is unaffected by whether s/he has previously made a witness statement or given evidence at the spouse's/civil partner's committal proceedings (*R v Pitt* [1983]). If the spouse/civil partner chooses to waive their right of refusal and give evidence against the spouse/civil partner defendant they become an ordinary witness, and having started their evidence they must complete it in the ordinary way.

If the defendant is on trial for more than one offence, only one of which is a compellable offence, then while the statute remains unclear, it is suggested that the spouse/civil partner will be compellable only on that offence (P. Creighton, 'Spouse Competence and Compellability' [1990] Crim. L.R. 34 at 39–41).

▶ R v L [2008]

Basic facts

The defendant's wife was sworn in by the prosecution but refused to state anything other than her name. Two questions arose: (1) do the police have a duty to caution the spouse when taking her statement that she is not compellable? (2) would admitting her hearsay statement circumvent s 80 PACE?

Relevance

The court held on (1) no need for a police caution for spouses as regards compellability, and (2) compelling a spouse to give evidence is not the same thing as permitting another witness to give (hearsay) evidence of her voluntary statement.

What if the defendant marries/enters a civil partnership in order to ensure that the spouse/civil partner cannot then testify against him/her?

▶ R (ON THE APPLICATION OF THE CROWN PROSECUTION SERVICE) v REGISTRAR GENERAL OF BIRTHS, MARRIAGES AND DEATHS [2003]

Basic facts

The defendant prisoner wanted to marry a key prosecution witness (she was the mother of his child) while awaiting trial for murder. By virtue of s 80 PACE, once married, she would cease to be a compellable witness for the prosecution. The question was whether the Registrar General could refuse or delay the marriage on applicable public policy grounds where such issue might facilitate the commission of, or avoidance of liability for, a serious crime.

Relevance

The court held that the marriage could not be refused or delayed, since everyone has the right to marry under Article 12 ECHR. Thus the court held it would not be contrary to public policy to issue the marriage certificate.

In any proceedings, a person who has been, but is no longer, married (or in a civil partnership) to the defendant shall be competent and compellable to give evidence as if that person and the defendant had never been married/in a civil partnership (s 80(5)). Marriage persists until grant of decree absolute (or dissolution of a civil partnership). Similarly, where an unlawful second marriage is undertaken the second spouse/civil partner is not taken to be a 'spouse'/'civil partner' and so is compellable (*R v Khan* [1987]).

By s 80A of PACE, the failure of a defendant's spouse/civil partner to give evidence shall not be made the subject of any comment by the prosecution. The judge, and counsel for any co-accused, can comment. In *R v Naudeer* [1984], the Court of Appeal said that, save in exceptional circumstances, a judge should exercise a great deal of circumspection if he chooses to make any comment. (The reason for this is that, as with any other potential witness, there may have been some good reason why that person was not called.) But counsel for a co-accused may, presumably, comment as strongly as he thinks fit.

CHILDREN IN CRIMINAL CASES

The current law is contained in ss 53–57 of the YJCEA. The fundamental provision is contained in s 53(1): at every stage in criminal proceedings all persons are, *whatever their age*, competent to give evidence. Although there is no minimum age for children to be assumed competent, very young children will often raise competency questions. The availability of special measures directions (below) can be taken into account in determining competency.

Assuming a child is competent to give evidence, will that child's evidence be sworn or unsworn? By s 55(2), no witness may be sworn unless:

(a) he has attained the age of 14; and

(b) he has a sufficient appreciation of the solemnity of the occasion and of the particular responsibility to tell the truth which is involved in taking an oath.

This is, in essence, the test applied in *R v Hayes* [1977], so belief in a divine sanction is unnecessary. Witnesses aged 14 and over, however, are likely to take the oath without further question because sub-s (3) provides that, if the witness is able to give intelligible testimony, he shall be presumed to have satisfied condition (b) if no evidence tending to show the contrary is adduced by any party. The effect of this is that children aged 14 and over will be treated as adults and no inquiry will be made into their capacity to take the oath unless an objection, supported by evidence, is made. If any question as to the satisfaction of either of the conditions in sub-s (2) arises, it is for the party wishing to have the witness sworn to satisfy the court that, *on a balance of probabilities*, those conditions are satisfied (s 55(4)). Again, the standard is the same for both the defence and prosecution, and the proceedings to determine the question will be conducted under the same rules as proceedings to determine competence (s 55(5)–(7)).

If a person is competent to give evidence, but fails to satisfy the tests for giving sworn evidence, his evidence may be given unsworn (s 56). The penalty for giving false unsworn evidence is the same as that of perjury for sworn evidence (s 57 YJCEA).

PERSONS OF IMPAIRED INTELLECT IN CRIMINAL CASES

Sections 53–57 of the YJCEA constitute a code governing the competence and capacity to be sworn of all persons tendered as witnesses in criminal cases. Where a potential witness has impaired intellect, therefore, the tests to be applied and the procedure for determining them are the same as have already been described in relation to children. It follows that a person with impaired intellect may be able to give evidence in criminal but not civil proceedings. In criminal proceedings, provided he satisfies the basic test for competence, he will be able to give evidence – if not sworn, then unsworn. Note that a simple failure to remember details is not the same as impaired intellect (*Director of Public Prosecutions v R* [2007] EWHC 1842 (Admin)). In civil proceedings, an adult witness with impaired intellect must be able to satisfy the *Hayes* test and be sworn; if he cannot do so, there is no provision enabling him to give unsworn evidence.

PROTECTING VULNERABLE OR INTIMIDATED WITNESSES

Sections 16–33 of the YJCEA provide for special measures to protect vulnerable or intimidated witnesses. Witnesses may be eligible for assistance, either on the grounds of age or incapacity under s 16, or on grounds of fear or distress about testifying under s 17. A witness is eligible under s 16 if he is under the age of 17 at the time of the hearing, or the court considers that the quality of evidence given by the witness is likely to be diminished because the witness suffers from a mental disorder or otherwise has a significant impairment of intelligence and social functioning, or the witness has a physical disability or is suffering from a physical disorder. Under s 17, a witness other than the accused is eligible for assistance if the court is satisfied that the quality of evidence given by the witness is likely to be diminished by reason of fear or distress on the part of the witness in connection with testifying in the proceedings. A complainant in respect of a sexual offence is also eligible for assistance in relation to proceedings in respect of that offence.

The court may make 'special measures directions' in respect of eligible witnesses under s 19.

> STEP 1: The court determines whether the witness is eligible for assistance under ss 16 and 17 YJCEA 1999.

> STEP 2: The court determines whether any of the available special measures (singly or in combination) would be likely to improve the quality of the witness' evidence.

> STEP 3: Under s 19(2) the court determines which of the special measures would be likely to maximise the quality of the witness' evidence.

It also has powers under s 21 to make special provisions for child witnesses, that is, witnesses under the age of 17 at the time of the hearing, if the trial is for one of the offences specified in s 35, which includes, *inter alia*, sexual offences and kidnapping. The primary rule in such a case is that evidence-in-chief must be video recorded and any evidence not given in that way must be given by means of a live link.

As well as video-recorded evidence and evidence by live link, the special measures available to the court include screening the witness from the accused, excluding the public from court (but only where the proceedings relate to a sexual offence or it appears to the court that there are reasonable grounds to fear intimidation of the witness), removal of wigs and gowns and examination through an interpreter or some other intermediary. As a final sweeping up provision, s 30 provides that a special measures direction may provide for 'such device as the court considers appropriate with a view to enabling questions or answers to be communicated to or by the witness despite any disability or disorder or other impairment which the witness has or suffers from'.

By s 32, where on a trial on indictment evidence has been given in accordance with a special measures direction, the judge must give the jury such warning (if any) as he considers necessary to ensure that the defendant is not prejudiced by that fact.

Sections 34–39 of the Act protect certain witnesses, such as complainants in trials for sexual offences and some child witnesses, from cross-examination by the defendant in person.

ADDITIONAL PROVISIONS UNDER THE CRIMINAL JUSTICE ACT 2003
Section 51(1) and (2) provides that a witness (other than the defendant) may, if the court so directs, give evidence through a live link:

- during a summary trial;

- at an appeal to the Crown Court arising out of a trial;

- at a trial on indictment;

- at an appeal to the Criminal Division of the Court of Appeal;

- at the hearing of a reference under s 9 or 11 of the Criminal Appeal Act 1995 (c 35);

- at a hearing before a magistrates' court or Crown Court which is held after the defendant has entered a plea of guilty; or

- at a hearing before the Court of Appeal under s 80 of this Act (s 80 deals with retrials (see Chapter 18)).

Section 51(3) provides that a direction may be given under this section on an application by a party to the proceedings, or of the court's own motion. Section 51(4) provides that a direction may not be given under this section, *unless*:

- a court is satisfied that it is in the interest of the efficient or effective administration of justice for the person concerned to give evidence in the proceedings through a live link;

- it has been notified by the Secretary of State that suitable facilities for receiving evidence through a live link are available in the area in which it appears to the court that the proceedings will take place; and

- that notification has not been withdrawn.

Section 51(6) provides that the court must consider all the circumstances of the case. Section 51(7) provides that this includes such things as the availability of the witness, the need for the witness to attend in person, the importance of the witness' evidence to the proceedings, the views of the witness, the suitability of the facilities at the place where the witness would give evidence through a live link, or whether a direction might tend to inhibit any party to the proceedings from effectively testing the witness' evidence. Section 51(8) further provides that the court *must* state in open court its reasons for refusing an application for a direction under this section and, if it is a magistrates' court, must cause them to be entered in the Register of Proceedings.

Section 54(1) provides that the judge may give the jury (if there is one) such direction as he thinks necessary to ensure that the jury gives the same weight to the evidence as if it had been given by the witness in the courtroom or other place where the proceedings are held.

When brought into force, ss 137 and 138 of the Criminal Justice Act 2003 will allow for certain witnesses to an offence triable only on indictment, or for a prescribed offence triable either way, to use their video-recorded statements in place of evidence-in-chief.

WITNESS ANONYMITY

The court retains an inherent power under the common law to control its own proceedings, which has led to the court varying the ways in which witnesses could give evidence. This was particularly useful before the introduction of statutory special measures directions. By a series of small steps, however, the courts reached a point in mid-2008 where they had allowed key witnesses for the prosecution to give evidence anonymously, ie without revealing their identity to the defendant or counsel. Just how successfully can a defendant challenge the credibility or evidence of an anonymous witness?

❯ R v DAVIS [2008]

Basic facts

Key prosecution witnesses were allowed to conceal their identity from the defendant, who denied murder. Anonymity was achieved using a combination of measures, including withholding of their names, addresses and personal details, and counsel was not permitted to ask questions which might enable identification. The defendant sought to challenge their credibility.

Relevance

The House of Lords found the protective measures imposed hampered the conduct of the defence in a manner and to an extent which was unlawful and rendered the trial unfair under Article 6 ECHR. Lord Mance commented that, 'in many cases, particularly cases where credibility is in issue, identification will be essential to effective cross-examination.'

The Criminal Evidence (Witness Anonymity) Act 2008 was speedily enacted following the judgment in Davis. Under s 2 the court can require 'specified measures' to be taken in relation to a witness as the court considers 'appropriate' to ensure that the identity of the witness is not disclosed, which can include:

(a) that the witness' name and other identifying details may be—
   (i) withheld;
   (ii) removed from materials disclosed to any party to the proceedings;

(b) that the witness may use a pseudonym;

(c) that the witness is not asked questions of any specified description that might lead to the identification of the witness;

(d) that the witness is screened to any specified extent;

(e) that the witness' voice is subjected to modulation to any specified extent.

Section 4 provides for three Conditions (Conditions A–C) to be satisfied before a witness anonymity order can be made:

Condition A, the measures specified in the order must be necessary to protect the safety of the witness or another person or to prevent serious damage to property, or to prevent 'real harm to the public interest' (s 4(3)). In deciding under Condition A, the court must have regard to any 'reasonable fear' on the part of the witness that if the witness were identified the witness or another person would suffer death or injury or there would be serious damage to property (s 4(6)).

Condition B, that having regard to all the circumstances, the taking of those measures would be consistent with the defendant receiving a fair trial (s 4(4)).

Condition C, it must be necessary to make the order in the interests of justice by reason of the fact that it appears to the court that it is important that the witness should testify, and the witness would not testify if the order were not made (s 4(5)).

When deciding whether Conditions A–C have been met the court is further directed by s 5 to have regard to a number of 'relevant considerations' (as well as 'such other matters as the court considers relevant'), such that:

(a) the general right of a defendant in criminal proceedings to know the identity of a witness in the proceedings;

(b) the extent to which the credibility of the witness concerned would be a relevant factor when the weight of his or her evidence comes to be assessed;

(c) whether evidence given by the witness might be the sole or decisive evidence implicating the defendant;

(d) whether the witness' evidence could be properly tested (whether on grounds of credibility or otherwise) without his or her identity being disclosed;

(e) whether there is any reason to believe that the witness has a tendency to be dishonest, or has any motive to be dishonest in the circumstances of the case, having regard to any previous convictions of the witness, and to any relationship between the witness and the defendant or any associates of the defendant;

(f) whether it would be reasonably practicable to protect the witness' identity by any means other than by making a witness anonymity order.

The considerations go primarily to the notion of fair trial, being based on issues such as the importance of the witness' evidence, its likely reliability, and the defendant's ability to challenge it (*R v Mayers*, *R v P* [2008]).

SPECIAL MEASURES DIRECTIONS FOR DEFENDANTS

The defendant is excluded from the special measures directions available under ss 16 and 17 of the YJCEA and the Criminal Justice Act 2003. This is so even where the defendant is a vulnerable child, although the trauma of the trial is mitigated in such circumstances by the child defendant being tried by a Youth Court. Section 33A of the Youth Justice and Criminal Evidence Act (as inserted by the Police and Justice Act 2006) now provides that defendants can give evidence via live link (but only live link) in limited situations where the use of this equipment will allow them to participate more effectively in the trial where their level of participation is compromised by levels of intellectual ability or social functioning (in the case of under 18s) or a mental disorder under the Mental Health Act 1983 (for adults).

You should now be confident that you would be able to tick all of the boxes on the checklist at the beginning of this chapter. To check your knowledge of Competence, compellability and special measures directions why not visit the companion website and take the Multiple Choice Question test. Check your understanding of the terms and vocabulary used in this chapter with the flashcard glossary.

5

The course of testimony

EXAMINATION–IN–CHIEF

This is the first stage in the examination of a witness at trial and is conducted on behalf of the party who has called him. In civil actions in the High Court, a witness' pre-trial written statement may stand as the evidence-in-chief (r 32.5 of the Civil Procedure Rules 1998).

A witness will often be favourable to the cause of the party calling him. Because of this, two rules that are peculiar to examination-in-chief have developed: the rules against leading questions and against discrediting one's own witness.

RULE AGAINST LEADING QUESTIONS

A leading question is one that suggests to the witness the answer that is wanted. An advocate may not generally ask leading questions of his own witness on matters that are in contention. This is because such a witness is thought likely to agree to suggestions made to him on behalf of a person to whom the witness is probably favourable.

A less usual, but always illegitimate, form of leading question is one that assumes that something has already been established by evidence when that is not the case. In *Curtis v Peek* [1864], the issue was whether a particular custom existed. The witness had not yet given evidence of that fact and it was held improper to ask whether certain conduct was in accordance with the custom, because that question assumed the custom to exist.

RULE AGAINST DISCREDITING ONE'S OWN WITNESS

A witness called by a party should have been put forward on the basis that he is honest. If a witness' evidence unexpectedly turns out to be contrary to the interest of the party who has called him, the latter cannot repair the damage by trying to show that the witness is of bad character (*Wright v Beckett* [1834] and s 3 Criminal Procedure Act 1865 applicable to both civil and criminal cases). But the party who has called the witness may, in such a case, call other witnesses to contradict the damaging testimony (*Ewer v Ambrose* [1825]). He may also, in some circumstances, show that the witness has previously made a statement inconsistent with the testimony given (*Greenough v Eccles* [1859]).

ORDER OF CALLING WITNESSES

There is no specific order in which parties must call witnesses in civil proceedings but in criminal proceedings it is usual for the defence to call the defendant as their first witness, if he intends to give evidence (s 79 Police and Criminal Evidence Act 1984). In criminal cases the Crown Court and Magistrates have the power to call and examine witnesses. The consent of the parties is not required but this is a power to be exercised rarely.

The general rule is that a party should adduce all its evidence before the close of that party's case and is ordinarily only permitted to adduce further evidence after closing where it was not previously foreseeable as being relevant to the party's case (*R v Day* [1940]).

CROSS-EXAMINATION

The objectives of cross-examination are to complete and correct the story told by a witness in examination-in-chief. Because of this, the right to cross-examine can be exercised by anyone whose interests have been affected by the testimony. Thus, co-claimants and co-defendants may cross-examine each other (*Lord v Colvin* [1855]; *R v Hadwen* [1902]). For the same reason, the scope of cross-examination is not confined to those matters dealt with during evidence-in-chief, but extends to all relevant matters (*Berwick-upon-Tweed Corp v Murray* [1850]).

Because the witness that is cross-examined may be unfavourable to the party cross-examining, there is no reason for a rule against leading questions. Since the cross-examining party has not been responsible for bringing the witness before the court, he does not vouch for the witness' character, and so may discredit him by all the proper means at his disposal.

But evidence obtained by cross-examination must still be admissible under the ordinary rules of evidence. Thus, a defendant must not be cross-examined about evidence that is inadmissible in relation to the case against him, even though it may be admissible in relation to a co-defendant, for example a confession.

CROSS-EXAMINING THE POLICE ON OTHER CASES

It was held in *R v Edwards* [1991] that police officers should not be asked about:

- untried allegations of perjury made against them, or about complaints not yet ruled on by the Police Complaints Authority;

- discreditable conduct by other officers, whether or not in the same squad.

An officer could, however, be asked about a case involving a different defendant, in which the officer had given evidence and in which the defendant had been acquitted, *where that acquittal necessarily indicated that the jury had disbelieved the officer's testimony*. But, in the absence of any reasons for a jury's verdict, this is an impossible test to satisfy. In *R v Meads* [1996], the Court of Appeal apparently approved a prosecutor's concession that defence cross-examination was permissible where a previous acquittal merely 'pointed to' fabrication of evidence by a police officer. The law remains unsettled. See *R v Guney* [1998], where *Edwards* was treated as binding authority but *Meads* was not cited.

CROSS-EXAMINATION ON PREVIOUS INCONSISTENT STATEMENTS

A witness may be cross-examined about an earlier statement of his that is inconsistent with his testimony in court. In civil proceedings, a previous inconsistent statement will be evidence of the truth of its contents (s 6(1) of the Civil Evidence Act 1995). Similarly, in criminal proceedings s 119(1) of the Criminal Justice Act 2003 provides that if a person gives oral evidence and he admits making a previous inconsistent statement, or a previous inconsistent statement made by him is proved by virtue of s 3, 4 or 5 of the Criminal Procedure Act 1865, the statement is admissible as 'evidence of any matter stated of which oral evidence by him would be admissible'. This phrase indicates that the evidence is being used in a hearsay manner (for the truth of the statement) and s 119 now allows previous inconsistent statements to be adduced as a specific exception to the hearsay rule, which is discussed further in Chapter 7.

The manner in which a witness should be cross-examined about previous inconsistent statements is governed by provisions in the Criminal Procedure Act 1865, which applies to civil as well as to criminal proceedings.

Section 4 applies to both oral and written statements (*R v Derby Magistrates' Court ex p B* [1996]) and is declaratory of the common law. It provides that, if a witness who has made a previous inconsistent statement does not 'distinctly' admit that he has done so, proof may be given that he did make it. Before such proof can be given, the circumstances of the supposed statement, sufficient to designate the particular occasion, must be mentioned to the witness. The 'circumstances' include, for example, details of the time of the earlier statement, the place where it was made and particulars of other persons present when it was made (*Angus v Smith* [1829]; *Carpenter v Wall* [1840]).

Section 5 applies to written statements only. Its effect is that a witness may be asked whether he made a statement and be cross-examined about its general nature without being shown the document. But, if the cross-examiner intends to use it as a contradictory statement, he must put it in evidence and the witness must be given the opportunity to explain the contradiction.

RE-EXAMINATION

The object of re-examination is to clarify and complete any matters referred to in cross-examination and left in an ambiguous or incomplete state. It is not permitted to ask questions in re-examination unless they arise out of matters dealt with in cross-examination (*R v Fletcher* [1829]).

REFRESHING MEMORY

'Refreshing memory' could refer to two different situations:

- where the witness' memory is actually jogged by the words on the page;
- where the events recorded were too long ago for the memory to be jogged, but the witness says that he is sure that the matters recorded are true (*Maugham v Hubbard* [1828]).

A witness can refresh his memory outside court, before giving testimony, by re-reading his witness statement. It is desirable, though not essential, for the prosecution to tell the defence if witnesses have done this (*R v Westwell* [1976]).

In civil cases the witness' statement will ordinarily stand as his evidence-in-chief, and due to the more relaxed rules on hearsay in civil proceedings refreshing memory from statements while giving evidence is allowed because the document will have already been admitted into court.

For criminal cases, s 139 of the Criminal Justice Act 2003 creates a presumption that a witness in criminal proceeding may refresh his memory while giving evidence from a document subject to two conditions: first, that he indicates that the document represents his recollection at the time he made it; and secondly, that his recollection was likely to be significantly better at the time the document was made by him (or verified by him). If the document has not been written by the witness it will need to have been verified, as an accurate account, by him. The simplest way of verification of the contents is by the witness signing the document (*Anderson v Whalley* [1852] where a ship's logbook although made by the mate was later checked and verified by the captain). Cases suggest verification may take place by the witness hearing the statements, although this will depend on all the circumstances. Contrast *R v Kelsey* [1981] where the officer read back the registration number to the witness and he agreed to its accuracy (although he did not see that this was actually what the officer had written down), with *R v Eleftheriou* [1993] where surveillance officers had two separate roles, one watching and calling out details while the other wrote them down. In *Kelsey* the court viewed the statement as having been verified but not in *Eleftheriou*.

The reference in s 139 to an 'earlier time' is generally believed to be a more relaxed concept than the previous common law notion of 'contemporaneous', and this appears to be reflected in the case law.

▶ R v McAFEE AND ANOTHER [2006]

Basic facts

The witness was a drug-taker and admitted to having told lies. The question was whether a statement made four months after the incident and just over a year before the trial could be used by her to refresh memory.

Relevance

The court held that the 'statute contains no requirement of contemporaneity'. It was for the judge to decide, having heard what the witness had to say, whether it was likely that her memory would have been significantly better at that earlier time or not (s 139(1)(b).

Section 120(3) of the 2003 Act is also relevant to documents used in this way. Where a statement made by a witness in a document is used to refresh memory while giving evidence he may be cross-examined on that statement. If the cross-examiner questions the witness on parts of the document not used by the witness to refresh his memory, the witness' party can request that the document as a whole is received into evidence. In this way the whole document will be shown to the jury. Where the document is received into evidence, s 120(3) makes the document admissible as evidence of the truth of the matter stated of which oral evidence by him would be admissible. This is a departure from the previous common law position, where the document would only have been admissible to demonstrate consistency (or inconsistency) of evidence.

The jury will receive a transcript of the evidence as an exhibit. According to s 122 Criminal Justice Act 2003, however, the jury will not be allowed to take the exhibit with them into the jury room (*R v Hulme* [2007]).

PREVIOUS CONSISTENT STATEMENTS

There is a general rule, sometimes referred to as 'the rule against narrative' or the 'rule against self-serving statements', that prohibits a witness from giving evidence that on some occasion before trial he made a statement that is consistent with his testimony at trial (*R v Roberts* [1942]).

▶ R v ROBERTS [1942]

Basic facts
The accused, charged with murder, claimed that the gun had gone off accidentally. He was not allowed to call evidence that two days after the shooting he had told his father that it was an accident. Such statements were excluded because they were hearsay, that is they were made otherwise than as oral evidence in court.

Relevance
At common law this case illustrates that previous consistent statements were usually excluded as they were hearsay, but also that they often add nothing to the evidence for a witness to suggest that they have previously said the same thing.

Despite this general rule there are exceptions where previous consistent statements are admissible. The exceptions can be split into (1) defendant and (2) other witnesses.

For defendants, it is the practice to admit statements made by an accused person to the police, even if they contain, either wholly or in part, an exculpatory element.

A wholly exculpatory statement, though not evidence of the truth of its contents, is admissible to show the attitude of the defendant at the time he made it. A wholly exculpatory statement would be one in which the defendant denied guilt. This is not limited to statements made on his first encounter with the police, though the longer the time that has elapsed since the first encounter, the less weighty the evidence is likely to be. It is the duty of the prosecution to present the case fairly, and it would be unfair to give evidence of admissions (which are admissible under s 76 of the Police and Criminal Evidence Act 1984), but exclude answers favourable to the defendant (*R v Pearce* [1979]).

A mixed statement (containing some inculpatory and some exculpatory parts) is also admissible. The judge should tell the jury to consider the whole statement when determining where the truth lies, but he should usually point out that excuses are unlikely to have the same weight as incriminating parts (*R v Sharp* [1988]). In *Sharp* the accused had admitted to being at the scene of the crime (a burglary) but said it was because he was looking for a part that had fallen off his car.

The difficulty is in knowing when a statement is 'mixed'. In *R v Garrod* [1997] the Court of Appeal held that a statement should only be regarded as 'mixed' if it contained an admission of fact which was 'significant' to the case, such as admitting an element of the offence.

▶ R v PAPWORTH AND ANOTHER [2007]

Basic facts

The Appellants were accused of conspiracy to defraud by dishonestly failing to disclose a relationship, negativing an arms-length business relationship. The two admitted to various aspects of a relationship but at all times denied any dishonesty and did not accept any ingredient of the offences charged.

> ### Relevance
> The court held that there were no admissions, either alone or cumulatively, which constituted a 'significant' admission. The court suggested that the question whether the admissions were 'significant' had to be answered by reference to what happens at the trial, not just what was said in interview, and can, therefore, only be finally resolved at the close of the evidence.

Purely inculpatory statements are defined as admissions or confessions and will be admissible (see Chapter 8).

For witnesses other than the defendant, previous consistent statements are admissible as exceptions to the general rule, in the following circumstances:

- To rebut an allegation of recent invention or fabrication (s 120(2) Criminal Justice Act 2003): rebuttal evidence is allowed by way of a previous consistent statement where it is suggested that a witness' evidence was fabricated at a particular point in time. The court must be able to pinpoint a specific time after which the witness' evidence is suggested to have been fabricated, and any statement consistent with that witness' oral evidence made before that time will be admissible. In *R v Oyesiku* [1971] to rebut the suggestion that the defendant's wife had prepared her evidence in collusion with her husband, she was allowed to adduce her statement to the same effect which she told to his solicitor after the defendant's arrest but before she had spoken with him. In *R v Tyndale* [1999] a child accused her mother's boyfriend of sexual assault. The defendant suggested that this was fabricated out of anger because he had been having an affair, but the child's previous statement was admissible since it was made before the discovery of the affair and, therefore, before she had a motive to lie.

- Where the statement is part of the *res gestae* (see Chapter 7).

- As evidence of previous identification (s 120(5)) Criminal Justice Act 2003: where the case includes a visual identification of a person and that identification is disputed, a witness' previous consistent statement showing that they have consistently identified the same person is admissible. The evidence is of value in such cases to negative the suggestion that the identification at trial is mistaken.

▪ Where the complainant to an offence has made a previous statement of complaint (s 120(7)) Criminal Justice Act 2003: the previous common law position referred only to recent complaints made in sexual offence cases (*R v Osborne* [1905]). The new provision in the 2003 Act broadens the scope of the offences to any offence where the person who made the complaint is the alleged victim. The criteria for admitting such complaints are listed in s 120(7)(8) and include;

(a) the witness claims to be a person against whom an offence has been committed,

(b) the offence is one to which the proceedings relate,

(c) the statement consists of a complaint made by the witness (whether to a person in authority or not) about conduct which would, if proved, constitute the offence or part of the offence,

(d) the complaint was made as soon as could reasonably be expected after the alleged conduct,

(e) the complaint was not made as a result of a threat or a promise, and

(f) before the statement is adduced the witness gives oral evidence in connection with its subject matter,

(g) for the purposes of subsection (7) the fact that the complaint was elicited (eg, by a leading question) is irrelevant unless a threat or a promise was involved.

Under the previous common law position for sexual offences only the case law showed a flexible approach to what was then required by way of a 'recent' or 'prompt' complaint. The value of a prompt complaint was that it was viewed to be more reliable than one made a long time after the alleged incident. The case law that built up, however, did allow for lengthier time delays depending on the circumstances, for example children might delay longer if they do not understand that it is wrong to be touched in a sexual way, or someone might delay until they have the chance to meet up with a specific friend. Under the new provision in s 120(7)(d) the time requirement is now 'as soon as could reasonably be expected', to which the courts appear to have taken a broad approach. In *R v K* [2008], also a sexual abuse case, the court allowed previous statements of complaint by a number of witnesses made many years after the alleged offences: some statements were made 20 years later. Such a broad reading of the new phraseology is to be welcomed, but admissibility will ultimately be a question for the court on the particular facts of the case. In *R v K* [2008] the court were of the view that 'of course, it was for the jury to reach conclusions as to the reasons for the delay in complaining, and the implications of that'.

There appears to be no limit to the number of statements of complaint that can be admitted (*R v O* [2006] where two were admitted), but there will be an issue of the evidential value of more than one statement. In order to be 'consistent' the previous statement does not need to be exactly the same as the oral evidence given at trial but it must usually disclose evidence of material and relevant conduct on the part of the defendant of the nature of the offence alleged (*R v S* [2004]).

▶ R v S [2004]

Basic facts

The complainant had not given the same details in her complaint to school friends (when aged 13/14) as at trial. At trial she alleged digital penetration, and vaginal and anal sexual intercourse, while in her statements to friends she had referred only to him having touched her, lain on top of her and put his hand up her night-dress. The question was the degree of consistency required for admissibility.

Relevance

The court held that this must depend on the facts, holding that it was not necessary that the complaint disclosed the ingredients of the offence but it must usually disclose evidence of material and relevant unlawful sexual conduct by the defendant.

Once the conditions in s 120 are satisfied the complainant will give evidence of the fact that she made a complaint and then the person to whom she made the complaint will give evidence of what the complaint involved (*White v R* [1999]).

For all statements to be adduced under s 120 Criminal Justice Act the witness will also need to fulfil s 120(4) that the witness indicates that to the best of his belief he made the statement, and that to the best of his belief it states the truth. Once adduced under s 120 statements are admissible as evidence of any matter stated. This is a significant departure from the previous common law position, under which previous consistent statements were admissible only to demonstrate consistency in the witness' evidence.

The jury will be directed in how to view such statements: 'a jury had to be directed not only that recent complaint was evidence of the truth of what had been stated, but that in deciding on the weight to give such evidence, they had to bear in mind that it comes from the same person who now makes the complaint in the witness box and not from some independent source' (*R v A* [2007]).

HOSTILE WITNESSES

A witness who fails to give the evidence expected of him may do so for honest reasons. Such a witness is merely 'unfavourable' and the advocate who calls him will have no remedy but to try to refresh his memory with his previous statement, or ultimately to call other witnesses to give a different account of events. But, if the witness fails to say what is expected because he is not desirous of telling the truth to the court at the instance of the party calling him, he will be a 'hostile witness'. In order to be treated as a 'hostile witness' the party calling the witness must seek the permission of the judge, based on his determination of the witness fulfilling the definition of 'adverse' (ie hostile). A witness ruled hostile by the judge may be cross-examined by the party calling him with a view to showing that he said something different on an earlier occasion (s 3 of the Criminal Procedure Act 1865; *R v Thompson* [1976]). Section 119 Criminal Justice Act allows previous inconsistent statements admitted by the witness or proved by virtue of s 3 Criminal Procedure Act 1865 to be adduced as 'evidence of any matter stated'. In this way, the jury can decide whether to believe the oral evidence given by the witness or the previous statement. In *R v Joyce and another* [2005] both before the trial and at trial three identifying eyewitnesses all retracted their statements, all testifying that they were mistaken as to the identity of the perpetrators of a shooting. In allowing them to be treated as hostile witnesses, undoubtedly on the basis of intimidation, the court emphasised that 'The shootings took place in broad daylight, at midday, in summer. The defendants were known to all three witnesses, who had unobstructed views of them, over a significant period of time; the suggestion that all three witnesses were initially confused or mistaken in the statements which they made on the day of these events strains credulity.' Once the previous inconsistent statements were adduced, the jury were free to choose which of the evidence to believe.

The witness may not, however, be cross-examined with a view to discrediting him by showing that he is of bad character. A judge may conclude that a witness is hostile without a *voir dire*; it is within his discretion whether to hold one or not (*R v Honeyghon and Sayles* [1999]).

▶ R v K [2007]

Basic facts
Having called 999 and requested police assistance against her husband for allegedly punching her, the complainant retracted her statement and refused to give evidence for the prosecution. Assuming that she would have been a hostile witness the prosecution chose not to call her but sought to adduce the contents of the 999 call.

Relevance
The court held that the process cannot be the subject of a shortcut, where the prosecution know she will be hostile they still need to call her, they cannot simply refuse to call her and expect that her (hearsay) witness statement will be admitted anyway.

CROSS-EXAMINATION OF COMPLAINANTS IN SEX CASES

The current law governing evidence of a complainant's extraneous sexual behaviour (where a sexual offence is alleged) is contained in ss 41–43 of the Youth Justice and Criminal Evidence Act 1999 (YJCEA). Section 41(1) puts a significant restriction on the way the defence can conduct its case where the defendant is charged with what the Act calls a 'sexual offence'. Note the ban does not include evidence tendered by the prosecution a[...]
(*R v Soroya* [2006]). The prosecution can lead with sexua[...]
and where they do the defence may be able to adduce e[...]
(if available) (see s 41(5)).

The concept of 'sexual offence' is defined in s 62 of the YJCEA to include all offences contained in the Sexual Offences Act 2003, and includes, among other offences, rape, indecent assault, unlawful sexual intercourse and any attempt to commit these offences.

The restriction imposed by s 41(1) is that, except with the leave of the court, no evidence may be adduced by the defence, nor any questions asked in cross-examination, 'about any sexual behaviour of the complainant'. 'Sexual behaviour' is defined in s 42(1)(c) as:

> . . . any sexual behaviour or other sexual experience, whether or not involving any accused or other person, but excluding (except in s 1n *R v Mukadi* [2004] it was held to be a matter of impression and common sense if a particular behaviour fulfilled the definition of 'sexual behaviour'. . . .

Note, the YJCEA, prima facie, prohibits defence questions about a complainant's previous sexual experience with the defendant as well as with others. In *R v Mukadi* [2004] it was held to be a matter of impression and common sense if a particular behaviour fulfilled the definition of 'sexual behaviour'. Such 'behaviour' has also been defined to include boasts and statements made about sexual behaviour (*R v W* [2004], *R v TW* [2005] both concerning statements of sexual encounters).

Questioning about sexual behaviour also includes 'sexual orientation'. In *R v B* [2007] the defendant was accused of male rape and pleaded consent, which implies that the complainant is a practising homosexual. The prosecution did not adduce any evidence as to the complainant's sexual orientation and the court held that s 41 prohibited the defence from adducing any evidence that the complainant was a practising homosexual. The court recognised that the issue of orientation was not always entirely irrelevant, since being homosexual would make it more likely that he may have consented but no more than that. The basis of the court's ruling seems to be that to permit the questions would be the same as to permit a woman (in a male–female rape) to be questioned as to previous sexual acts, to establish that she would be more likely to consent if she was experienced sexually.

What does not amount to questions about sexual behaviour is an allegation of 'se accusations where the defendant can sufficiently evidence the lie without needing to question the complainant or others about sexual matters. In *R v MH* [2002] it was held that the defence must, if such cross-examination is to be permitted, have a proper evidential basis for asserting that the previous statement was made and that it was untrue. An acquittal or a decision by the police or complainant not to pursue the case have been held as generally not sufficient evidence to demonstrate 'a proper evidential basis' (*R v D* [2007], *R v V* [2007], but see *R v Garaxo* [2005]). In *R v Murray* [2009] the court explained 'proper evidential basis' as 'less than a strong factual foundation for concluding that the previous complaint was false. But there must be some material from which it could properly be concluded that the complaint was false'.

If a 'proper evidential basis' is shown the question can be asked outside of the s 41 regime as the question is deemed not to be about 'sexual behaviour' but about a clearly evidenced lie. For example, in *R v V* [2007] the complainant admitted to her step-sister that the complaint was false, and so either the step-sister could have been called as a witness or the complainant's previous inconsistent statement could have been adduced if she testified inconsistent with it. If a 'proper' evidential basis for the lie is not available the court would need to analyse the sexual behaviour issues raised and so s 41 is applicable, requiring an admissibility exception.

By s 41(2), the court may give leave to adduce evidence of the complainant's sexual behaviour, or to allow cross-examination about it if, and only if, it is satisfied of two matters: first, that either sub-s (3) or sub-s (5) applies; and, second, that a refusal of leave might have the result of rendering unsafe a conclusion of the trier of fact on any relevant issue in the case (*R v Bahador* [2005]).

The expression 'any relevant issue in the case' is defined by s 42(1)(a) as 'any issue falling to be proved by the prosecution or defence in the trial of the accused'. Under s 41(4) evidence or questions will not be held to relate to a 'relevant issue' if the purpose, or main purpose, for adducing it is to impugn the credibility of the complainant.

> ## ▶ R v MARTIN [2004]
>
> ### Basic facts
>
> The defendant denied having sexual intercourse with the complainant. He argued that her false accusation of rape was based on revenge for his earlier rejections of the complainant following some sexual conduct with her.
>
> ### Relevance
>
> In seeking to evidence prior sexual conduct with the complainant, while *one* purpose might have been to impugn the credibility of the complainant, the court held that it was not *the* purpose or indeed the *main* purpose. It was emphasised that the sexual nature of the earlier incident went to the strength of the complainant's reaction at being rejected by the defendant and therefore to the plausibility of the defence case.

Finally, the evidence or questions must relate to a specific instance(s) of alleged sexual behaviour of the complainant (s 41(6)).

THE CATEGORIES OF ADMISSIBILITY: SUB-SECTIONS 3 AND 5

Sub-section 41(3) applies if the evidence or question in cross-examination relates to a relevant issue in the case and either:

(a) that issue is not an issue of consent; or

(b) it is an issue of consent, and the sexual behaviour of the complainant to which the evidence or question relates is alleged to have taken place at or about the same time as the event which is the subject matter of the charge; or

(c) it is an issue of consent and the sexual behaviour of the complainant is alleged to have been, in any respect, so similar–

  (i) to any sexual behaviour of the complainant which the defendant alleges took place as part of the event which is the subject matter of the charge; or

  (ii) to any other sexual behaviour of the complainant which the defendant alleges took place at or about the same time as that event,

  that the similarity cannot reasonably be explained as a coincidence.

THE SCOPE OF SUB-SECTION (3)(a) 'NOT AN ISSUE OF CONSENT'

This sub-section distinguishes between cases where the evidence or question in cross-examination relates to a relevant issue, but that issue is not one of consent, and those cases where the relevant issue *is* one of consent. The expression 'issue of consent' is defined in s 42(1)(b) as 'any issue whether the complainant in fact consented to the conduct constituting the offence with which the accused is charged (and accordingly does not include any issue as to the belief of the accused that the complainant so consented)'. So, if the defence is not that the complainant consented, but that the defendant *reasonably but mistakenly believed that she was consenting*, the test is whether the evidence or question relates to a relevant issue in the case, provided always that the complainant's history provides a reasonable basis for believing he or she consented (*R v A (No 2)* [2001]).

But the test of relevance where such a defence is put forward has been strictly applied. In *R v Barton* [1987], the defence to a rape charge was mistaken belief that the complainant had consented. The defendant wanted to call evidence of the complainant's sexual experiences with other men to establish the foundation for that belief, but the trial judge refused leave. The Court of Appeal upheld this decision and drew a distinction between belief that a woman *would consent if asked* and belief that a woman *is consenting* to a particular act of intercourse.

Other issues falling under the category as 'not issues of consent' include issues of identification, and denial of the alleged act having taken place at all (*R v Martin* [2004]). Also evidence and questions about the complainant's previous sexual history with other men may be relevant because of the specific inferences they permit which point to the accused's innocence. For example, in *R v Viola* [1982] the defendant wanted to evidence that the complainant had had sexual intercourse with other men very soon after the alleged incident. The inference that he was trying to draw was that in having sex so soon after the alleged rape the woman was not in the pain that she indicated she was. As Lord Craighead in *R v A (No 2)* [2001] also said, such evidence and questions may show that the complainant was biased against the accused or had a motive to fabricate the evidence, or that there is an alternative explanation for the physical conditions the prosecution are relying on to prove that intercourse took place.

▶ R v F [2005]

Basic facts

The defendant was accused of sexually abusing his step-daughter (when they were both adults). The complainant had suggested that she was an unhappy and unwilling partner. The accused's defence was that the complainant had fabricated the allegations, because he had chosen to end their adult consensual relationship and she was not happy with this.

Relevance

Photographic evidence showing the pair happy was admissible under s 41(3)(a) as relevant to the defence of false accusation out of revenge and because the evidence was inconsistent with the complainant's allegation of domination following childhood abuse.

THE SCOPE OF SUB-SECTION (3)(b) 'AN ISSUE OF CONSENT' AND ACTS TAKING PLACE AT THE SAME TIME AS INCIDENT (*RES GESTAE*)

Sub-section (3)(b) allows the court to look, but only to a limited extent, at the context in which the event which is the subject matter of the charge is alleged to have taken place. The timeline of 'at the same time' was an issue in the seminal House of Lords case of *R v A (No 2)* [2001]. While in *R v Mokrecovas* [2002] the court had no difficult in holding that evidence of sexual behaviour in the same evening might be relevant as 'at the same time', the House of Lords in *R v A (No 2)* [2001] had to decide upon a gap of three weeks. The case is detailed below, but on the matter of the timeline the House decided that three weeks was too long a gap for the provision to allow. Their Lordships interpreted the phrase differently, some suggesting only a day or 48 hours at most, while the most extreme view was one week either side of the alleged incident. Consequently, any sexual behaviour longer than a week before or after the alleged incident will be difficult to evidence under sub-section (3)(b).

THE SCOPE OF SUB-SECTION (3)(c) 'AN ISSUE OF CONSENT' AND SEXUAL BEHAVIOUR 'SO SIMILAR'

Sub-section (3)(c) allows the court to look at the sexual behaviour of the complainant on other occasions where that behaviour is so similar to the behaviour of the complainant on the occasion under investigation that the similarity cannot be explained as a coincidence. The behaviour may match either some element alleged by the defendant to have been part of the event that has led to the charge, or some feature of its surrounding circumstances within the limitations just described. It also appears to cover behaviour either before or after the alleged offence.

This category of admissibility might be useful in adducing evidence which challenges some generalisation of behaviour that the jury might otherwise assume, for example, that a very young girl would not have sexual intercourse with much older men, or group sex, or sex in a public place. In *R v T* [2004] the alleged sexual behaviour was concerning sexual intercourse in a climbing frame in a children's outdoor play area. In referring to a similarity 'that cannot reasonably be explained as a coincidence', the House of Lords in *R v A (No 2)* [2001] were clearly of the opinion that the evidence must go beyond what is 'commonplace' (which is how they viewed the 'normal sexual relationship' suggested by the defendant) in order to be relevant.

▶ R v A (No 2) [2001]

Basic facts

The defendant, accused of rape, alleged consent (and also ran the defence of mistaken belief in consent). The defendant alleged that the two had been having a consensual sexual relationship, the last such sexual behaviour having taken place three weeks before the alleged rape. The evidence was held to be admissible under s 41(3)(a) where the defendant ran the mistaken belief in consent defence, but it would not have been admissible had he not ran that defence; hence, it was not admissible as having taken place 'at the same time' or as being 'so similar to behaviour on other occasions'. The defence raised the question of the compatibility of s 41 in this latter scenario with the right to a fair trial under Article 6 of the European Convention.

> **Relevance**
> The House of Lords read into the Act a judicial discretion to admit the evidence though s 41 where the evidence is nevertheless so relevant to the issue of consent that to exclude it would endanger the fairness of the trial under Article 6 of the Convention. If this test is satisfied the evidence should not be excluded.

SUB-SECTION (5) REBUTTAL OF PROSECUTION EVIDENCE

Sub-section 41(5) applies where the prosecution adduces evidence about any sexual behaviour of the complainant, and the evidence to be adduced or the question to be asked by or on behalf of the accused relates to the prosecution evidence and goes no further than is necessary to rebut or explain it. Note s 41(4) restricting evidence impugning the character of the complainant is not applicable to evidence given in rebuttal under s 41(5).

This exception to the general prohibition applies if the evidence or question relates to any evidence adduced *by the prosecution* about any sexual behaviour of the complainant. So, if during examination-in-chief the complainant states that she was a virgin before she was raped, the defence may cross-examine with the object of rebutting that assertion and call evidence to do so if need be.

What is meant by 'adduced by the prosecution' was addressed in *R v Hamadi* [2007], where the court was of the opinion that evidence deliberately elicited from the complainant in cross-examination would not generally fall within the definition of 'adduced by the prosecution'. Such evidence would, therefore, need to fulfil the admissibility requirements of a different exception to be adduced. If, however, the complainant freely gave the information in cross-examination (say without prompting or hard questioning) then this could fall within the terms of 'adduced by the prosecution'.

In *R v Tilambala* [2005] the defendant was charged with rape. The defendant sought to introduce evidence that the complainant, contrary to her suggestion that she was faithful to her boyfriend, had contemplated going back to a stranger's flat. The court held that the interpretation which the accused wished to place on this evidence is that the complainant was a girl who was prepared to go back to the house of the man in the bar, in order to engage in sexual activity. That, the court held, is clearly precluded by s 41; otherwise it was not relevant since it only showed that she had previously thought about going back to a man's house and on this occasion with the defendant she did.

SUB–SECTION (6)

This provides that, for the purposes of sub-ss (3) and (5), the evidence that is permitted to be called must relate to specific instances of alleged sexual behaviour by the defendant.

PROCEDURE

By s 43, an application for leave under s 41 shall be heard in private and in the absence of the complainant. Nothing is said of the defendant's presence; presumably, Parliament did not intend to exclude him, and the application will be made to the court after members of the press and public have been excluded. Where such an application has been determined, the court must state in open court, but in the absence of the jury if there is one, its reasons for giving or refusing leave and, if leave is granted, the extent to which evidence may be adduced or questions asked. Presumably, this will also take place in the presence of the defendant, but in the absence of the complainant, who would otherwise be alerted to questions that she would face in cross-examination.

See flow chart overleaf.

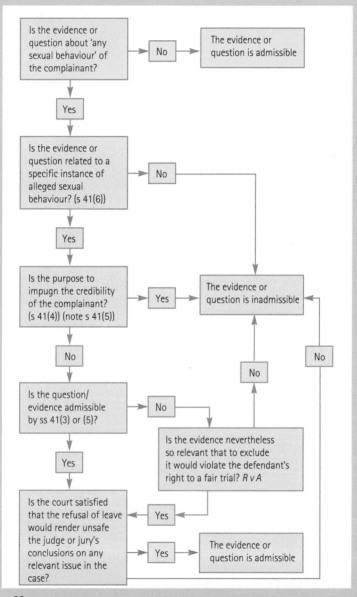

COLLATERAL QUESTIONS

Questions put to witnesses must be relevant to either a fact in issue in the case or a collateral matter, for example an issue of credibility of a witness to suggest to the fact-finder that the witness should not be believed or that the witness' evidence should not be trusted. This distinction is often difficult to make, particularly in sexual offence cases where issues of credibility are often closely intertwined with the facts in issue in the case. A good example is provided by *R v Burke* [1858] where an Irish witness claimed not to be able to speak English. This claim was questioned in cross-examination, where the cross-examiner sought to evidence that he had spoken English to two persons in court, which he denied. The court held this to be a collateral matter, since his ability to speak English was not a fact in issue in the case, merely a way to question the credibility of the witness in suggesting that he had lied to the court. Had the case concerned whether the witness had made a specific statement which was in English his ability to speak English would have likely been a fact in issue, rather than merely a collateral matter, and the answer then could have been rebutted.

When questions or evidence relate to such credibility issues (as collateral matters) a witness' answers to such questions are said to be 'final', in the sense that evidence may not subsequently be adduced to rebut the answer given by the witness. This is known as the rule of finality. The reasoning of the rule is to prevent the trial descending into a trial of collateral matters. Accepting the answer as final does not mean that the answer is true, merely that the cross-examiner is prohibited from adducing evidence of rebuttal. Note, however, the following exceptions.

■ By s 6 of the Criminal Procedure Act 1865, a witness' previous convictions may be proved where he denies them or refuses to answer. Since the Criminal Justice Act 2003 introduced changes to the admissibility of bad character evidence (including convictions) of both defendant and other witnesses, ss 100 and 101 of that Act will now determine if a question about bad character (convictions) can be 'lawfully' asked of a witness. Similarly, being 'lawfully' questioned includes issues under the Rehabilitation of Offenders Act 1974.

■ If a witness denies that he is biased, either for or against a party, evidence may be called to disprove him (*R v Mendy* [1976]). Again since an allegation of bias also probably falls within the definition of 'bad character' or 'reprehensible behaviour' for ss 100 and 101 Criminal Justice Act 2003, those provisions must determine the evidence of bias to be admissible also.

■ Evidence may be given of a witness' general reputation for untruthfulness such that he is not worthy of belief (*R v Richardson and Longman* [1968]); evidence may be given to show the witness has tailored his evidence to reflect another witness' evidence. Again, if the untruthfulness also makes the evidence fall within the remit of ss 100 and 101 of the Criminal Justice Act 2003 admissibility will need to be sought under those provisions also.

■ Medical evidence may be given of a physical or mental disability affecting the reliability of a witness' evidence (*Toohey v Metropolitan Police Commissioner* [1965]).

You should now be confident that you would be able to tick all of the boxes on the checklist at the beginning of this chapter. To check your knowledge of The course of testimony why not visit the companion website and take the Multiple Choice Question test. Check your understanding of the terms and vocabulary used in this chapter with the flashcard glossary.

6

Identification evidence

Judges in the past attempted to control the way in which juries thought about kinds of evidence that were regarded as particularly unreliable. Early informal rules of practice later developed into formal rules of law about directions that should be given during a summing up. One of these sets of rules came to be known as the law relating to 'corroboration' which required juries to be warned about the danger of convicting on the 'uncorroborated' evidence of a witness in three types of case: where the witness was an accomplice, a child, or a complainant in a case where a sexual crime was alleged. The law of corroboration has now been very largely abolished by s 34(2) of the Criminal Justice Act 1988 (in relation to the evidence of children) and s 32 of the Criminal Justice and Public Order Act 1994 (in relation to evidence of accomplices and of complainants in sexual cases). The effect of these sections was stated by the Court of Appeal in *R v Makanjuola* [1995] to be that trial judges now have a wide discretion to adapt warnings about the testimony of any witness to the circumstances of the case. But for a warning to be given, there must be some *evidential* basis for suggesting that the witness' testimony may be unreliable.

Despite the existence of this modern discretion, a body of case law has developed concerning warnings that a judge may be *bound* to give to the jury concerning identification evidence.

IDENTIFICATION AND *TURNBULL* GUIDELINES

In *R v Turnbull* [1977], the Court of Appeal laid down guidelines for judges summing up in cases where the prosecution relies on contested identification evidence. Failure to follow the guidelines is likely to lead to the quashing of a conviction as unsafe. The *Turnbull* guidelines include a cautionary warning to the jury to the effect that witness identification evidence can be mistaken. But why? Evidence shows that a witness' initial perception and later recall of a stranger's facial features are not generally reliable. This unreliability can be exacerbated by any circumstances at the scene of the original perception and by subsequent methods of recall.

▶ R v SHERVINGTON [2008]

Basic facts
The victim made some inconsistencies in how he described the mugger and identified the defendant two and a half months after

the assault. The judge wrongly suggested that the jury use their common sense when considering identification evidence and suggested that they avoided an 'over-sophisticated approach to the identification evidence' which he described as resulting in a 'mugger's charter'.

Relevance

The Court held that while the *Turnbull* direction should be appropriately tailored to the case, it is rarely appropriate to depart in this way from the basics of that direction. It is exactly what *Turnbull* warns against; otherwise people would view as reliable the identification evidence of a convinced witness.

WHEN DO THE GUIDELINES APPLY?

They apply whenever the prosecution case depends 'wholly or substantially' on the correctness of one or more identifications of the defendant, and the defence alleges that the identifying witnesses are mistaken.

A *Turnbull* direction must also be given in cases where identification is based on recognition (recognition is where the witness purports to know the person, rather than identification of a stranger (*Freemantle v R* [1995])) as well as in other situations where there is a more obvious risk of error (*Shand v R* [1996]). In *Shand v R* [1996] it was suggested that the witness was not mistaken but lying; still the court required a *Turnbull* direction to the jury in case they rejected the suggestion of a false identification they must still be aware of the possibility that the witness was in fact mistaken.

The need for a *Turnbull* direction generally arises where the issue is whether the defendant was present at a particular place or not. Where his presence at the scene is not disputed, but his participation in the offence is, the direction does not have to be given automatically. It will be necessary to give it where there is the possibility that the witness has mistaken one person for another, for example, because of similarities of clothing, colour or build (*R v Slater* [1995]), or because of confused action (*R v Thornton* [1995]). In *R v Slater* [1995] the defendant denied assault but admitted being in the pub at the time where the assault took place. Here a *Turnbull* direction was deemed not necessary as due to the defendant being the only very tall person in the bar it was unlikely he had been mistakenly identified. In *R v Thornton* [1995], however, a *Turnbull* direction was seen as necessary where the assault took place at a wedding reception where people were dressed similarly to the defendant and so there was a possibility of mistaken identity.

The cases in which a *Turnbull* warning can be wholly omitted will be exceptional. A *Turnbull* direction almost certainly does not have to be given where evidence pointing to the accused is not evidence of *identification*, but only evidence of description, for example, where the witness observes only distinctive clothing or the general appearance of a suspect, such as his height and build (*R v Gayle* [1999]). Similarly, the warning of mistaken identification applies only to human faces and so the *Turnbull* direction is not needed where a witness identifies a vehicle, for example (*R v Browning* [1992]).

Finally, a *Turnbull* direction is not appropriate where the jury is invited to make an identification themselves from photographs or video recordings taken at the scene of the crime.

WHAT DOES A *TURNBULL* DIRECTION REQUIRE?

A judge giving a *Turnbull* direction must do three things:

- warn the jury of the special need for caution before convicting the defendant on the evidence of identification;

- tell the jury the reason why such a warning is needed. Some reference should be made to the fact that a mistaken witness can be a convincing one, and that a number of such witnesses can all be mistaken. *R v Pattinson* [1996] suggests that there should be a reference to the risk of miscarriages of justice resulting from mistaken identifications;

- tell the jury to examine closely the circumstances in which each identification came to be made. But it is not necessary in every case for the judge to summarise for the jury all the weaknesses of the identification evidence. If he does choose to summarise that evidence, he should point to strengths as well as weaknesses (*R v Pattinson* [1996]).

The circumstances of the identification will include the weather (was it raining? foggy? a clear day?); whether there were any obstructions in the witness' view; the length of time the witness viewed the suspect; the length of time before the witness gave a description of the suspect; whether the witness was in distress (was a weapon involved?); whether the suspect was wearing anything to conceal his features; the distance between the witness and the suspect.

It was said in *R v Turnbull* [1977] that, where the quality of the identification evidence is good, the jury can safely be left to assess it without any supporting evidence, subject to an adequate warning; but, where the quality is poor, the judge should withdraw the case from the jury at the end of the prosecution case unless there is other evidence to support the correctness of the identification. The importance of the *Turnbull* direction was affirmed in *R v Ley (Kerry)* [2007] where an appeal against a conviction for aggravated burglary was dismissed. The court held that the trial judge had adequately covered the weaknesses in identification and it was for the jury to consider as part of the evidence.

Good identification evidence might involve a long observation of the suspect in good conditions, or a shorter observation of someone well known to the witness. Poor identification evidence tends to include 'fleeting glimpses' of the suspect; a very short observation of a stranger, for example, in stressful and dark conditions. If the judge views the identification evidence as poor, he must look for supporting evidence that suggests that the defendant has been correctly identified. And having warned the jury in accordance with the *Turnbull* direction, as developed in later cases, the judge should go on to direct the jury to consider whether the identification evidence is supported by any other evidence, identifying for them the evidence that is capable of providing such support.

Such supporting evidence may include circumstantial evidence placing the accused at the scene (eg fingerprints, DNA, CCTV footage), items found on the defendant or in his possession when arrested (eg the stolen items), evidence of motive, or a false alibi (as evidence of the defendant's lies).

EVIDENCE OF THE DEFENDANT'S LIES

Evidence of lies told by a defendant inside or outside court can have probative value, but will often require a direction from the judge to ensure that the jury approaches such evidence with care. The court must give a jury direction in line with the decision in *R v Burge* [1996], such that:

■ the lie must be admitted by the defendant, or the jury must find it proved beyond reasonable doubt, before the jury can take it into account;

■ the jury must be warned that the mere fact that the defendant has lied is not in itself evidence of guilt, because defendants may lie for innocent reasons. Only if the jury is sure that the defendant did not lie for an innocent reason can a lie support the prosecution case. The effect of this is that the prosecution has to negative any innocent explanation for the defendant's lie before the jury can take it into account in deciding whether the case is proved.

According to *R v Burge* [1996], a direction on these lines is usually required in four situations:

■ where the defendant relies on an alibi;

■ where the judge suggests that the jury look for something to support a possibly unreliable item of prosecution evidence, and points to an alleged lie by the defendant as potential support;

■ where the prosecution tries to show that the defendant has told a lie, either in or out of court, about a matter apart from the offence charged, but which points to the guilt of the defendant on that charge;

■ where the jury might adopt such an argument, even though the prosecution has not used it.

But a *Burge* direction is not required in every case where a defendant testifies merely because the jury might conclude that he told a lie about something while on oath. A direction will not be required where rejection by the jury of something the defendant said will leave them no choice but to convict. This will be the case where the prosecution evidence is in direct and irreconcilable conflict with the defendant's evidence on a matter central to the case (*R v Harron* [1996]), and may thus include in some cases, despite what was said in *R v Burge*, a lie about an alibi. In *R v Middleton* [2000], the Court of Appeal dismissed an appeal on the basis that to have given the direction would have confused the issue for the jury.

VOICE IDENTIFICATIONS AND *TURNBULL*

A *Turnbull* direction will also be necessary in cases of voice identification, where the witness purports to identify the suspect on the basis of having heard their voice. Cases of voice identification are rare and tend to suffer from greater risks of misperception than do facial identifications. Thus in *R v Roberts* [2000] the court suggested that in cases of voice identification the *Turnbull* warning should be given in even stronger terms than ordinarily.

In *R v O'Doherty* [2002] the prosecution suggested that it was the defendant's voice recorded in a phone call to the emergency services. The defence were allowed to adduce expert evidence in voice recognition, who suggested that two tests are required; auditory phonetic analysis which focuses on dialect or accent, and quantitative acoustic analysis which measures the differences in acoustic properties of the person's speech (dependent on individual vocal tract, mouth and throat). The state of science in this area suggests that voice identifications, even from recorded sources, are not without their evidential limitations in court.

IDENTIFICATIONS INSIDE AND OUTSIDE COURT

Identification evidence may be in a number of forms, including DNA or fingerprint evidence or dock identifications, but the more likely scenario that includes an identifying witness requiring a *Turnbull* direction will be where a witness sees the perpetrator and subsequently identifies the suspect using the police identification procedures under PACE Code of Practice C.

EVIDENCE OF PREVIOUS IDENTIFICATIONS

The evidence of a previous out of court identification of the defendant can be given by the person who made the identification, because it shows that the witness was able to identify the defendant at a time nearer to the events under investigation, so reducing the chance of mistake *R v Christie* [1914]).

The rule against hearsay has been relaxed to allow evidence to be given by an observer (eg a police officer) of someone else's out of court identification, even where the witness who made the original identification has failed to remember in court that she identified anybody (*R v Osbourne and Virtue* [1973]). Previous identifications would now fall within the admissibility criteria of s 120(3) Criminal Justice Act 2003.

CODE D OF PACE

In order to bolster the reliability of witness identifications PACE introduced a number of procedural obligations on police when a witness purports to be able to identify the perpetrator. These procedures are contained in PACE Code of Practice C, and, while not a statutory provision, breaches of the Code are likely to result in the exclusion of either the identifying evidence or possibly other evidence obtained as a result of that breach. Exclusion of evidence is governed by s 78 PACE, since breaches of the Code are likely to diminish the reliability of the identification evidence and may affect the fairness of the proceedings. Exclusion of evidence is not automatic on breach of the Code (*R v Kelly* [1998]).

The Code states that the procedures 'are designed to *test* the witness' ability to identify the person they saw on a previous occasion'. In addition, safeguards for the defendant were included in the Code to increase the likelihood that the identifying evidence is as reliable as possible and to protect the defendant from the possibility of mistaken identification. Thus the first safeguard for a defendant is that generally whenever a suspect disputes identity as the offender the police must hold an identification procedure. There are two exceptions 'where it would serve no useful purpose in proving or disproving whether the suspect was involved in committing the offence', such as where:

■ the suspect is already well known to the witness and does not dispute this fact;

■ there is no reasonable possibility of the witness making an identification (possibly where the witness did not see the person's face (*R v Oscar* [1991])).

Specifically, where a breach relates to a failure to hold an identification parade, the court in *R v Forbes* [2001] held that the jury should be told that holding an identification procedure allows the accused to test the reliability of the identification witness' evidence and that in not holding such a procedure the accused has thus been denied the benefit of the safeguard which an identity procedure provides. The jury should be directed to take this factor into account and to give such weight to this as they think fair.

Before a suspect becomes 'known' to the police the procedures for finding him are more relaxed, but must still follow certain procedures to ensure reliability of evidence. A suspect becomes 'known' when there is 'sufficient information known to the police to justify the arrest of a particular person for suspected involvement in the offence' (Code D, paragraph 3.4). In order to have a known suspect the police may drive the witness around the area where the incident happened, if sufficiently recently that the perpetrator might still be present, to try to find him, or the police may search for the perpetrator themselves, based on the witness' description of him. In addition, the police may show the witness police photographs to see if the witness can identify the perpetrator from them. Annex E of Code C governs the showing of police photographs to witnesses. But the fact that this means of identification has been adopted should not usually be brought out at trial by the prosecution because of what it will reveal about the defendant's background (*R v Lamb* [1980]). The regulations in Annex E include:

- The first description of the suspect given by the witness must be recorded by the police before any photographs or e-fits, etc are shown to the witness.

- Only one witness can be shown photographs, etc at a time.

- The witness must be shown a set of 12 photographs at a time.

- The witness will be told that the photograph, etc of the person they saw may or may not be amongst those shown.

- The photographs shown must be of a similar type.

- The witness must not be prompted in any way or guided in her choice.

- If a witness makes a positive identification from the set of photographs no other witness can be shown the set and all witnesses should be asked to attend an identification procedure (the suspect does not then dispute identity).

- If a witness makes a selection but is unable to confirm the identification, the witness will need to indicate how sure they are in that selection.

- The photographs must be retained for evidential purposes later at the trial.

Once the suspect becomes 'known' to the police the procedures become more formal, but similar requirements to Annex E are used to promote accuracy of identification and reliability of evidence. If the defendant is 'available' (largely meaning 'willing' and present in the area) to take part in a procedure he will be informed of certain information (under paragraph 3.17), including the purposes of the identification procedure, his entitlement to free legal advice and the right to have a solicitor or friend present. Most importantly, the suspect will be told that they do not have to consent to take part in a procedure but that if they do not consent that there are two possibilities: first the refusal to co-operate will be given in evidence at a future trial, and secondly, the police may use images taken of the suspect covertly to proceed with an identification.

The defendant will ordinarily be offered to take part in a video identification, regulated by Annex A of Code C. Video identification is now the preferred format, largely due to ease and cost. The witness will be shown a set of nine recorded images of persons, who resemble the suspect in terms of 'age, height, general appearance and position in life', posing in the same positions or carry-ing out the same sequence of movements, including the defendant. If the suspect has an unusual physical feature on their face, for example a facial scar, tattoo, or distinctive hairstyle or hair colour, steps must be taken to conceal it on the suspect or replicate it on the others images, possibly digitally. Additional safeguards are also provided in that the defendant's solicitor should be shown the set of images first and given the chance to object to the use of any particular image in the set, witnesses are not allowed to communicate with each other and are not reminded of the descriptions provided by them or told if any other witness has made any identification, and each witness must view the video at least twice before making any identification.

If a video procedure is not available alternative procedures are the identifica-tion parade (Annex B), group parade (Annex C) and confrontation (Annex C). These other procedures have similar safeguards to those of the video parade but confrontation is the least desirable mechanism for identification. A 'con-frontation' is when the suspect is directly confronted by the witness, who is asked if this is the perpetrator. A group parade involves the use of a location, usually a shopping centre, where the suspect is situated among a range of persons who may not closely resemble the suspect.

THE EFFECT OF BREACH OF THE CODE

The Code contains many intricate provisions on keeping witnesses apart while making their identifications and ensuring that all images in the procedure resemble the suspect, for example. Thus where the police breach one of the provisions of the Code this may have an effect on the accuracy or reliability of the identification evidence obtained. Breaches of Code D, therefore, may result in the exclusion of identification evidence in the exercise of the trial judge's discretion under s 78 of PACE. The judge should exclude such evidence if it is felt that its admission would have an adverse effect on the fairness of the proceedings (*R v Quinn* [1995]).

Where the breach was carried out in bad faith the court is more likely to exclude the evidence under s 78. But where the breach was not in bad faith the judge will take into account the strength of the other evidence in the case linking the defendant to the crime (implicating the defendant). Therefore where the other evidence is strongly incriminating, the 'fairness of the proceedings' threshold is unlikely to be met. If the other evidence only slightly incriminates the defendant, and thus the identification evidence obtained by breaching the Code is the sole or main prosecution evidence, then fairness may be significantly affected by its admission and the judge may be minded to use his discretion to exclude that evidence.

Where, however, a trial judge admits identification evidence in the context of such breaches, he should draw the breaches to the attention of the jury so that the jury can decide what, if any weight to give to the identification evidence in light of the breaches (*R v Forbes* [2001]; *R v Quinn* [1995]; *R v Khan* [1997]). The type of direction will vary depending upon the particular circumstances of the case and the nature of the specific breach of Code D.

In *R v Finley* [1993] the witness identified the defendant from the police photographs two weeks after the robbery. The defendant was a blonde skin-head and the other photos were of dark haired men (a violation of the Code). An identification parade was held for the witnesses who had been kept together beforehand (in violation of the Code). At the identification parade the other men were of heavier build than the defendant and again had dark hair (breaching the Code). The defendant produced an alibi and there was no other evidence linking him to the robbery. On the basis of the many breaches of the Code and the lack of any other incriminating evidence the court excluded the identification evidence under s 78.

▶ R v MARCUS (2004)

Basic facts

The defendant was accused of a number of robberies. The suspect was described as a 'black man in his late thirties or forties with greying hair and a greying beard'. In agreement with the defendant and his solicitor, the police, having difficulties in finding eight other persons (on the 19,000 strong database) who resembled the defendant, decided to mask the hair and beard features on the images. In addition, the police created a second set of images which were not masked and included people who did not resemble the defendant (most in their twenties and only two had any facial hair). Unsurprisingly, most of the witnesses picked out the defendant in the unmasked version, some did in the masked version but were hesitant.

Relevance

The police admitted that because of the appearance of the other volunteers the defendant would, 'blatantly stand out' and that the procedure was 'blatantly unfair'. Unsurprisingly the court viewed the police actions as a 'deliberate device to evade the provisions of the Code. That falls to be condemned by this court'. The court suggested that nowadays the police may be able to use digital masking which might be an improvement.

VOICE IDENTIFICATIONS

There is little authority on this subject but the Code specifically suggests that it does not preclude the police making use of aural identification procedures where they judge it appropriate. In *R v Hersey* [1998] the witness purported to identify a suspect in the robbery of his shop. Although the robbers were wearing balaclavas, the witness thought he identified the voice of one of the robbers as a long-standing customer. He did so from 12 voices. While the expert viewed 12 voices as being too many, he also suggested that the other voices in the line-up were of a higher pitch than the defendant. But the court upheld the decision of the trial judge to allow the evidence.

In *R v Roberts* [2000] the judge was wrong to allow a voice identification by the Polish victim who only heard her attacker in a 'snippet' of conversation in circumstances of fear. Expert evidence suggested that in these circumstances there was a high likelihood of mistaken identification.

DOCK IDENTIFICATIONS

It has been said that identification of a defendant for the first time when he is in the dock at trial is to be avoided (*R v Cartwright* [1914]). But, in *Barnes v Chief Constable of Durham* [1997], the Divisional Court acknowledged that such evidence was acceptable in magistrates' courts in certain cases.

You should now be confident that you would be able to tick all of the boxes on the checklist at the beginning of this chapter. To check your knowledge of Identification evidence why not visit the companion website and take the Multiple Choice Question test. Check your understanding of the terms and vocabulary used in this chapter with the flashcard glossary.

7

Hearsay

DEFINITION OF HEARSAY

Hearsay is one of the most important rules of the law of evidence. The seminal case of *R v Kearley* [1992] defined hearsay as 'an assertion other than one made by a person while giving oral evidence in the proceedings and tendered as evidence of the matters stated.' Taken together ss 114 and 115 Criminal Justice Act 2003 produce the following four criteria for hearsay:

1   a statement of fact;
2   made by a person other than while giving evidence in the proceedings;
3   tendered in order to prove the truth of some fact asserted in it (the truth of the matter stated);
4   made to cause a person to believe the matter or a person or machine to act on the matter as stated.

The exclusionary rule is based on the repetition in court of a statement made outside of court, possibly even spoken by the witness himself, when that statement is being used to demonstrate the truth of some fact asserted in it. The purpose for admission of statements is therefore paramount; if it is not being adduced for the truth of the fact then it does not fall within the hearsay exclusionary rule and will be admissible in the ordinary way if relevant.

▶ R v GIBSON [1887]

Basic facts

After an argument with the victim's son in a pub, it was alleged the defendant threw the stone which wounded the victim. The victim did not see the defendant throw the stone, but an unidentified woman did and pointed to a door saying 'the person who threw the stone went in there.' The police arrived and arrested the defendant in that house.

Relevance

At the trial a police officer sought to give the statement, not the unidentified woman. The statement was being tendered for its truth, that the identity of the perpetrator was the defendant in that he did actually did go into that particular house (and in which the accused was found). Held: inadmissible hearsay.

The basis for the exclusionary rule is the principle of orality, in that the jury should be basing their verdict on what they hear live in the courtroom by witnesses present to testify to what they saw. Other exclusionary rationales include: that the hearsay statement was not originally given on oath and so there being no guarantor of its veracity; the absence of cross-examination and the difficulty of assessing the weight of hearsay; the missed opportunity to assess the demeanour of the witness who made the statement; the risk of mistaken transmission or fabricated evidence; and the right of the defendant to confront his accusers. Of these rationales possibly the most convincing today is the risk of mistaken perception, of a witness mishearing or misinterpreting what he heard.

In *Teper v R* [1952] the court gave the reasoning for the hearsay rule: 'The rule against admission of hearsay evidence is fundamental. It is not the best evidence and it is not delivered on oath. The truthfulness and accuracy of the person whose words are spoken by another witness cannot be tested by cross-examination, and the light which his demeanour would throw on his testimony is lost.'

The hearsay rule was abolished for civil cases in 1995 but remains a central exclusionary rule in criminal cases. For civil cases, therefore, any weaknesses in the hearsay evidence will go to its weight, rather than its admissibility.

Before the criminal law rule was overhauled in the Criminal Justice Act 2003, the general rule demanded the exclusion of hearsay evidence unless it fitted within a particular exception. Exceptions to the exclusionary rule were to be found in the common law and statute. Where an exception could not be found the evidence was excluded. And so a rule based on promoting live witness testimony did not always engender the most reliable evidence. A good example is presented by the case of *Myers v DPP* [1965] where valuable documentary records were held to be inadmissible hearsay. Here the rule required evidence of the employee who documented the vehicle identification numbers (VIN number) of the cars rolling off the production line three years earlier. While the employee would have been able to refresh his memory from the document he made at the time, it was in fact the document that was more likely to contain the true picture than the recollections of the workers after three years. While Parliament acted quickly to legislate for the admittance of documentary hearsay, judical 'fudging' of the issue often occurred with new exceptions being created on the spot for what the court perceived to be very valuable evidence.

While most of the common law and statutory exceptions to exclusion have been maintained under the Criminal Justice Act 2003, two aspects in particular have revolutionalised the criminal justice approach to hearsay evidence. The first major change is the new inclusionary rule contained in s 114(1)(d), where the judge may allow hearsay evidence where he believes the interest of justice requires such admission. The second change is found in s 115 which, in short, removes the notion of 'implied statements' from the definition of hearsay.

CRIMINAL JUSTICE ACT 2003 DEFINITION OF HEARSAY

s 114 Criminal Justice Act 2003 stipulates the exclusionary rule, such that:

'In criminal proceedings a statement not made in oral evidence in the proceedings is admissible as evidence of any matter stated if, but only if . . .'

s 115 adds:

2   A statement is any representation of fact or opinion made by a person by whatever means; and it includes a representation made in a sketch, photofit or other pictorial form.
3   A matter stated is one to which this Chapter applies if (and only if) the purpose, or one of the purposes, of the person making the statement appears to the court to have been
     (a) to cause another person to believe the matter, or
     (b) to cause another person to act or a machine to operate on the basis that the matter is as stated.

Note that the word 'statement' or 'assertion' covers all forms of human communication, not just spoken. And so the concept can include statements that are written, oral or by gestures (*Chandrasekera v R* [1937] where the victim, whose throat had been cut, was able to nod to indicate the perpetrator). Section 115(2) also reverses the previous position on photofits. The court in *R v Cook* [1987] had viewed photofits as akin to photographs and so not falling within the hearsay rule. There is a clear admissibility exception for such photofits, however in s 117(4) (more later).

Section 115(2) refers to a statement by a 'person', and so statements made wholly by a computer or automated machine will fall outside the exclusionary rule and so will be admissible if relevant, in the normal way (note s 129).

IMPLIED STATEMENTS

For a statement to constitute hearsay there must be some 'fact' asserted in it. The statement, 'the car is blue' contains the fact that the car was a particular colour, whereas screams do not ordinarily contain a fact.

The definition of 'a matter stated' in s 115(3) has narrowed down the definition of hearsay by largely removing what were known as implied statements from its ambit (*R v Singh* [2006]). Section 115(3) defines hearsay to include an intentional element to the communication, in causing another person to believe the matter or a person or machine to act on that matter (*R v N* [2006]).

What was an implied assertion? An implied assertion was when a particular meaning was inferred by the witness from the statement or conduct of another person. A good example was provided in *Teper v R* [1952], where the defendant's shop burnt down and he was charged with arson. At the scene of the fire an unidentified woman in the crowd was heard to say 'Your place is burning and you are going away from the fire'. The woman was not called as a witness, but instead the police officer sought to adduce her statement; at issue was her statement of (possibly mistaken) identification of the defendant in the car driving away from the fire and the inference that he was suspiciously fleeing the scene, possibly having set the fire himself. The court viewed the woman's statement as hearsay and excluded it.

The court in *Wright v Doe d. Tatham* [1837] referred to the now infamous example of the deceased ship's captain who carefully examined a ship before embarking on it with his family. The court created a hypothetical example to illustrate the difficulties in using such evidence. The ship's captain having carefully examined the ship then sets sail in it with his family, whereupon it sinks and they all die. In answering the question whether the ship was seaworthy, one might infer from his conduct in examining the ship and setting sail on it with his family as akin to a statement of its seaworthiness. That being so, the court held it would (under the old law) have constituted hearsay. In truth we would not know for sure why the captain set sail on that ship, or whether he did in fact believe the ship to be seaworthy. And this indicates some of the problems with implied assertions; such evidence is often even more replete with uncertainties than is hearsay.

In the case of *R v Kearley* [1992] the House of Lords rejected as hearsay the implied assertions of drug dealing in the statements by callers to the defendant's house asking for drugs. None of the callers were called to give evidence and the court refused to admit evidence of the police officers who heard the requests. The judgment in *Kearley* was a 3:2 majority split, the majority holding the evidence of the implied statements of the callers (implying that they believed the defendant to be a drug dealer) to be hearsay and irrelevant as showing only the callers' belief. The minority, on the other hand, thought the evidence could be used circumstantially to demonstrate that the callers were customers of the defendant.

What of implied assertions today? With the inclusion of an intentional element requirement in s 115(3) most implied statements will be excluded from the definition of hearsay, and so a close analysis must be made of such statements to determine the specific purpose of the statement. But if not within the hearsay definition then such statements will be admissible in the normal way if relevant to the proceedings (see *R v Singh* [2006] where at issue were phone numbers stored in the call register of a mobile phone). The recent case of *R v N* [2006] confirms this position with respect to a diary, being intended to be read or actioned by anyone, but the more recent case of *R v K* [2007] takes this approach a step further.

▶ R v K [2007]

Basic facts

The defendant was charged with multiple counts of gross indecency of a child and rape of a female under 16. The complainant had written in her diary about the incidents charged. She had since burned the diary but her aunt had read it and sought to recount its contents to the court.

Relevance

The court again stated that a diary is not hearsay (and so admissible) referring instead to the diary as direct evidence and so in viewing the diary the aunt's reading is akin to her seeing the robber run away from the scene of the crime.

While implied assertions generally no longer constitute hearsay their admissibility will be determined on the basis of relevance (provided always that no other exclusionary rule is infringed). It is possible that due to the side issues that an implied statement may entail it may fail the relevance test and any such statements admitted into evidence will need careful treatment by the jury.

ADMITTED FOR ITS TRUTH

The wording of s 114 refers to 'is admissible as evidence of any matter stated' which essentially refers to the truth of the fact asserted. Thus statements only constitute hearsay if they contain a fact which it is contended is true; if another reason is provided for the admission of the statement into evidence the hearsay rule will not be engaged. Other reasons to adduce a statement could include: to prove that it was made, to prove the way in which it was made (threatening, calmly), or to prove the effect it had on another person (felt threatened, felt fear). In *Subramaniam v Public Prosecutor* [1956] the defendant was charged with the unlawful possession of ammunition and his defence was duress. He tendered evidence of the duress in the form of statements of threats made to him. The court held that the statements were not hearsay as they were not tendered to prove that the terrorists would actually carry out their threats but in order to show (1) that the threats were made, and (2) the defendant's state of mind as a result of them.

STATEMENTS PROVING THE NON-EXISTENCE OF AN ALLEGED FACT

In some situations a statement is made by a fact not being included in a document where one would otherwise expect it to be included. For example, if the Government compile a list of legal migrants, the absence of a particular name on that list (while known to be in the country) would suggest that the person was an illegal immigrant (*R v Patel* [1981]). But is it hearsay to rely on the absence of an item from the list? In *Patel* the court held that the person who made the document or who knew how it was compiled should be called, therefore it was hearsay.

STATEMENTS WHICH ARE LIES

In *Mawaz and Amarat Khan v R* [1967] alibi statements by the defendants were suggested to be lies and were admissible. The statements were not hearsay because they were not being adduced to prove the truth of what was said but the opposite.

ADMISSIBILITY CATEGORIES OF HEARSAY EVIDENCE

Section 114(1) Criminal Justice Act 2003 provides that a *statement* not made in oral evidence in criminal proceedings is admissible as evidence of *any matter stated* provided that:

(a) any provision of this Chapter (chapter 2) or any other statutory provision makes it admissible;

(b) any rule of law preserved by section 118 makes it admissible;

(c) all parties to the proceedings agree to it being admissible, or

(d) the court is satisfied that it is in the interests of justice for it to be admissible.

Leaving aside the exception that all parties agree to admission, there are three major ways in which hearsay evidence may be admissible: statute, a preserved rule of the common law or the new inclusionary rule. The exceptions to the exclusionary rule are largely based on the statement having been made in circumstances that suggest reliability or where to exclude the statement would mean excluding the only evidence available.

HEARSAY AS THE SOLE OR DECISIVE EVIDENCE

The Court of Appeal remain of the view that the hearsay regime provided by the Criminal Justice Act 2003 contains sufficient counterbalancing factors to ensure that where hearsay evidence is admitted as the sole or decisive evidence in the case this will not breach the defendant's right to a fair trial under Article 6 ECHR (*R v Al-Khawaja* [2006]; *R v Horncastle, Marquis and Carter* [2009]). This is not, however, the view of the European Court of Human Rights where in the recent case of *Al-Khawaja and Tahery v United Kingdom* [2009] the Court held that the constituent right to confrontation in Article 6(3)(d) is an 'express guarantee' in itself and must be met before going on to consider if the trial as a whole is fair. The court did allow for exception in the situation where fear of the defendant is the reason the absent witness refuses to attend court (see s 116(2)(e) below). The Court of Appeal in *Horncastle* have

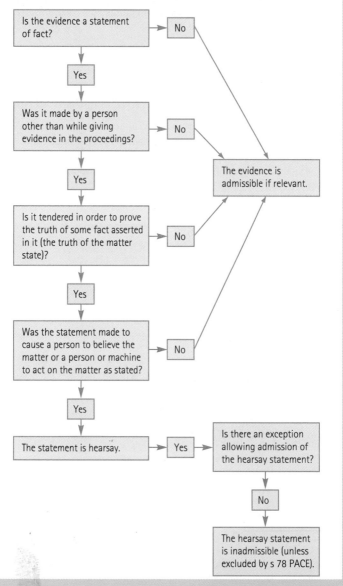

since rejected the European Court's judgment, but the issue remains a live one for hearsay cases where the sole or decisive evidence is that of an absent witness.

STATUTORY EXCEPTIONS

SECTION 116: CASES WHERE A WITNESS IS UNAVAILABLE

Under s 116(1) a statement is admissible as evidence of any matter stated, provided that that person's *oral* evidence would have been admissible, that the maker of such a statement (the relevant person) is identified to the court's satisfaction and that any of the five *conditions* as discussed below is satisfied.

CONDITIONS – s 116(2)

The conditions are:

(a) that the relevant person is dead;

(b) that the relevant person is unfit to be a witness because of his bodily or mental condition (see *R (on the application of Louis Meredith) v Harwich Justices* [2006]);

(c) that the relevant person is outside the United Kingdom and it is not reasonably practicable to secure his attendance;

(d) that the relevant person cannot be found although such steps as is reasonably practicable to take to find him have been taken;

(e) that through *fear* the relevant person does not give (or does not continue to give) oral evidence in the proceedings, either at all or in connection with the subject matter of the statement, and the court gives *leave* for the statement to be given in evidence.

The relevant person is dead or unfit

Where a witness to an alleged crime died before trial, the admission of their statement made for the purposes of any prosecution is allowed on the basis of necessity. Similarly, where a witness is suffering from a physical or mental condition which would allow them to attend court, but would put them at risk of further complications their hearsay statement can be admitted. In *R v Setz-Depsey* [1994] and *R v Millett* [2000] the court viewed the provision (formerly s 23(2)(a) Criminal Justice Act 1988) as covering the witness' ability to give meaningful testimony when actually in court. The court will require proof of the condition (*R (on the application of Louis Meredith) v Harwich Justices* [2006]).

> ▶ **R v COLE AND ANOTHER (KEET) [2007]**
>
> ### Basic facts
> The defendant was charged with attempting to obtain property by deception. The only witness was an 82-year-old lady who suffered from dementia.
>
> ### Relevance
> Despite being the only evidence in the case the hearsay statement made when she was not suffering from dementia could be admitted as an exception to the hearsay rule. The court went further, however, and (unnecessarily) considered the criteria relevant to the inclusionary rule in s 114(1)(d) and whether the interests of justice required the statement's admission.

The relevant person is outside the United Kingdom

The term 'reasonably practicable' should be judged on the basis of the steps taken, or not taken by the party seeking to secure the attendance of the witness. The court should also consider whether to exercise its exclusionary powers under 126 of the Act or s 78 PACE 1984. Whether it was fair to admit such statements would depend partly on what efforts should reasonably be made to secure the attendance of the witness, or at least, to arrange a procedure whereby the contents of the statements should be clarified and challenged (*R v C and another* [2006]).

In *R v Castillo* [1996] the court stated that the judge must consider the following general factors to determine whether it is reasonably practicable to secure attendence:

- the importance of the evidence the witness could give;

- the expense and inconvenience of securing attendance; and

- the weight to be given to the reasons put forward for non-attendance;

- the seriousness of the offence itself (eg is the defendant's liberty at stake?);

- the extent of the prejudice it would cause to the defendant were the absent witness' statement read out, affording no opportunity to cross-examine.

These factors were cited with approval in the case of *R v Gyima* [2007] EWCA Crim 429 where the American parents of the witness (aged 14) would not cooperate in bringing the boy back to the UK to give evidence. The court questioned whether the prosecution had done enough to secure his attendance, or at least his evidence, possibly by using a live link.

This issue of making an assessment of whether the party had taken sufficient steps to secure the evidence of the witness was raised in the conspiracy case of *R v C and K* [2006] where an important prosecution witness in South Africa refused to give evidence. While the Prosecution had a sworn witness statement, the court held that insufficient attempts had been made to allow the defence to challenge the statement; the court suggested that a procedure be set up in South Africa where the prosecution and defence could question the witness. This case shows that the party must go to some lengths to obtain the evidence rather than use hearsay.

The person could not be found
The party will need to prove that all reasonable steps have been taken to find the person but that he cannot be found. Leaving a phone message on the witness' answering machine is not 'all reasonable steps to find him' (*R v Adams* [2007]).

Fear
For the purposes of sub-s (2)(e) 'fear' is widely construed and includes fear of the death or injury of another person or of financial loss. And the source of the fear or its basis is irrelevant (*R v Martin* [1977]). To admit a hearsay statement in circumstances of fear the court give leave, and can only do so where its admittance would be in the 'interests of justice' (s 116(4)). In granting leave the court must have regard to the statement's contents, any risk that its admission or exclusion will result in unfairness to any party to the proceedings, to the possibility of making a special measures direction under section 19 YJCEA for the witness, and to 'any other relevant circumstances'. It must be

proven to the court that the witness is genuinely in fear, possibly by admitting evidence of the witness' state of mind, or by taking evidence by way of live link. It is not thought permissible to call the witness to the full court to give evidence of their fear as this would be likely only to compound it (*R v Davies* [2006]).

Where a court is sure that a witness does not give evidence through fear, then a statement made by the witness may be admitted, even though the evidence may be the sole evidence against the defendant; but the court must be sure to examine the quality and reliability of the evidence (*Sellick v Sellick* [2005]).

SECTION 117: BUSINESS AND OTHER DOCUMENTS

Under s 117(1), a statement contained in a document is admissible as evidence of any matter, provided that such oral evidence would have been admissible, that the requirement of sub-s (2) is satisfied, and the requirements of sub-s (5) are satisfied, in a case where sub-s (4) requires them to be.

SUB-SECTION (2)

2   The requirements of this section are satisfied if:
   (a) the document or part containing the statement was created or received by a person in the course of a trade, business, profession or other occupation, or as the holder of a paid or unpaid office;
   (b) the person who supplied the information contained in the statement (the relevant person) had or may reasonably be supposed to have had personal knowledge of the matters dealt with; and
   (c) each person (if any) through whom the information was supplied from the relevant person to the person mentioned in paragraph (a) received the information in the course of a trade, business, profession or other occupation, or as the holder of a paid or unpaid office.

SUB-SECTION (4)

The additional requirements of sub-s (5) must be satisfied if the statement was prepared for the purposes of pending or contemplated criminal proceedings, or for a criminal investigation, but was not obtained pursuant to a request under s 7 of the Crime (International Co-operation) Act 2003 (c 32) or an order under para 6 of Sched 13 to the Criminal Justice Act 1988 (c 33) (which relates to overseas evidence).

SUB-SECTION (5)

The requirements of this sub-section are satisfied if any of the five conditions mentioned in s 116(2) are satisfied, or the relevant person cannot reasonably be expected to have any recollection of the matters dealt with in the statement (having regard to the length of time since he supplied the information and all other circumstances).

The rationale for the admittance of documents generated in the course of business as exceptions to the hearsay rule is due to the general perception of their accuracy and reliability (*Myers v DPP* [1965]). Section 117 does not require that the original statement was *made* in a document, just that it was contained in a document. And so the original statement could have been made orally and written down in a document during the course of a trade or business. The major requirement for this admissibility exception is that every link in the chain must involve someone receiving or creating the document in the course of trade or business.

Where the statement was prepared for the purposes of pending or contemplated criminal proceedings, or for a criminal investigation, an additional requirement is needed: that the witness who made the statement fulfils one of the absence criteria for s 116 or the additional requirement that 'the relevant person cannot reasonably be expected to have any recollection of the matters dealt with in the statement (having regard to the length of time since he supplied the information and all other circumstances)'. The absence criteria demonstrates the law's preference , where possible, for the witness' evidence to be given in court rather than simply admitting the hearsay statement.

Although s 117 is subject to the overall exclusionary discretion in s 126, the provision contains a specific exclusionary rule in s 117(6)(7) based on the poor quality of the hearsay statement. Under s 117(7), the court may decide that a statement is not admissible if it is satisfied that the statement's reliability as evidence for the purpose for which it is tendered is doubtful in view of:

(a) its contents;

(b) the source of the information contained in it;

(c) the way in which or the circumstances in which the document concerned was created or received.

SECTION 118: PRESERVED COMMON LAW EXCEPTIONS

The following common law categories are preserved by s 118 of the Criminal Justice Act 2003 and so may be admissible in evidence.

1 PUBLIC INFORMATION

This is admissible as evidence of the facts stated in them. For example, published works dealing with matters of a public nature (such as histories, scientific works, dictionaries and maps); public documents (such as registers, and returns made under public authority with respect to matters of public interest); records (such as the records of certain courts, treaties, Crown grants, pardons and commissions). Evidence relating to a person's age or date or place of birth may also be given by a person without personal knowledge of the matter.

2 REPUTATION AS TO CHARACTER

Evidence of the accused's general reputation in the community is admissible for the purpose of proving his good or bad character. Evidence of good character is relevant to the accused's guilt, that is, because he is of good character he is unlikely to have committed the offence. Similarly, evidence of bad character appears relevant to the accused's guilt, that is, because he is of bad character he is more likely to have committed the offence.

3 REPUTATION OR FAMILY TRADITION

Evidence of reputation or family tradition is admissible for the purpose of proving or disproving pedigree or the existence of a marriage, the existence of any public or general right, or the identity of any person or thing.

4 *RES GESTAE*

The Latin expression '*res gestae*' may be loosely translated as 'events occurring' or 'things happening'. If a statement is said to be part of the *res gestae*, what is meant is that it is an out of court statement so closely associated with the circumstances in which it was made as to guarantee a greater reliability than usual. The rationale of this common law hearsay exception was provided by Grove J in *Howe v Malkin* [1878], such that:

'Though you cannot give in explanation a declaration per se, yet when there is an act accompanied by a statement which is so mixed up with it as to become part of the res gestae, evidence of such a statement may be given.'

Such a statement is admissible as evidence of the matter stated if:

- the statement was made by a person so *emotionally overpowered* by an event that the possibility of concoction or distortion can be disregarded;

- the statement accompanied an act which can be properly evaluated as evidence only if considered in conjunction with the statement; or

- the statement relates to a *physical sensation* or *mental state* (such as intention or emotion).

Emotionally overpowered

This category is also often referred to as 'excited utterances'. These are spontaneous exclamations of the victim of an offence or of an observer. Although most of the cases are victims' utterances, this exception is not confined to them (*Milne v Leisler* [1862]). Most of the case law turns on the proximity in time of an utterance to some 'exciting' incident, usually an attack on the victim. The excitement of being attacked or having one's throat slit is deemed to overtake the mind of the victim to the extent that what he said while still in the throes of excitement (possibly in identifying his attacker) will likely be reliable. A good example is provided by *R v Bedingfield* [1878] where the defendant (Harry Bedingfield) was charged with murder. As his victim crawled into another room, her throat cut, she uttered, 'Look what Harry's done!' and promptly died. The hearsay statement would fall within the *res gestae* exception (as well as s 116 now).

In order to ensure greater reliability of the truth of the statement the court in *R v Andrews* [1987] laid down the test for admissibility as follows:

- the primary question that the judge must ask is whether the possibility of concoction or distortion by the original speaker can be disregarded;

- to answer that question, the judge must first consider the circumstances in which the particular statement was made, in order to satisfy himself that the event was so unusual, startling or dramatic as to dominate the thoughts of the speaker to the extent that his utterance was an instinctive reaction to that event, giving no time for reasoned reflection. In such a situation, the judge would be entitled to conclude that the involvements or pressure of the event excluded the possibility of concoction or distortion, provided the statement was made in conditions of approximate contemporaneity;

- for the statement to be sufficiently spontaneous, it must be so closely associated with the startling event that the mind of the speaker was still dominated by that event. The fact that a statement was made in answer to a question is only something to be taken into consideration under this head; it does not mean that the statement will inevitably lack sufficient spontaneity;

- quite apart from the time factor, there may be special features in the case that relate to the possibility of concoction or distortion by the original speaker, for example, a motive of fabrication. Where a feature of this kind exists, the judge must be satisfied that there was no possibility of any concoction or distortion to the advantage of the speaker or the disadvantage of the defendant;

- the ordinary fallibility of human recollection may affect the weight of the testifying witness' evidence, but is not relevant to the question of *admissibility*. There may, however, be special features giving rise to the possibility of error, for example, where the original speaker was drunk, or had made identification in particularly difficult circumstances. If there are special features such as these, the judge must consider whether he can still exclude the possibility of error before admitting evidence;

- where the trial judge has properly directed himself as to the correct approach to the evidence, and there is material that entitles him to reach his conclusions, the Court of Appeal will not interfere with his decision.

In *Andrews* the victim was stabbed in his home during a burglary and managed to make his way to the flat below and name the perpetrators to the police. But the victim had been drinking heavily on the occasion in question, increasing the possibility of mistaken identification. The victim died two months later and his hearsay statement was adduced in evidence.

An Andrews checklist

- Was the nature of the event such as to make what was said an instinctive reaction to it?

- How close in time were the words of the event?

- Were there any special features to suggest that the original speaker might have given a *dishonest* account of the event?

- Were there any special features, apart from the fallibility of ordinary memory, to suggest that the original speaker might have given a mistaken account of the event?

Obviously, an 'excited utterance' argument cannot succeed where the utterance precedes that dramatic event by a significant period of time. See *R v Newport* [1998], where the utterance preceded the dramatic event by 20 minutes.

The nature of the event itself and the lapse of time between the event and the statement are likely to feature in arguments about admissibility. The less dramatic the event, and the greater the lapse of time, the less likely it will be that the speaker's mind was still dominated by the event, so as to rule out any opportunity for concoction or distortion.

Compare *Tobi v Nicholas* [1987] concerning a minor road accident and a statement given 20 minutes later (held not *res gestae*) and *R v Carnall* [1995] where the victim was badly beaten and stabbed, the statement identifying his perpetrators being given an hour later after he crawled for help.

In *Attorney-General's Reference (No 1 of 2003)* [2003] it was held that a judge had no discretion to exclude evidence falling under the *res gestae* just because there was better service available.

> ▶ ATTORNEY-GENERAL'S REFERENCE (No 1 of 2003)
>
> Basic facts
>
> The defendant was charged with causing grievous bodily harm to his mother. The mother refused to testify truthfully and the prosecution sought to bypass her untruthful testimony by adducing her hearsay statements made to witnesses who had heard her call out, saw her in distress and heard her identify the defendant as her

attacker. The issue was whether this evidence could be admitted under the *res gestae* exception to the hearsay rule.

Relevance

The Court of Appeal reiterated that there is no witness unavailability requirement for *res gestae*, but in not giving the defence the opportunity to cross-examine the witness the judge may use his discretion to exclude the evidence under s 78 of PACE.

Statements accompanying and explaining the relevant act

Under this hearsay exception the statement is admitted because it accompanies a legally significant act, such that the statement explains the purpose for the act (*R v Bliss* [1837]). The criteria for this exception are that the statement:

1 relates directly to the act;
2 was made contemporaneously with the act; and
3 that the actor made it.

    (a) Therefore the maker of the statement and the person performing the act must be the same person.

    (b) The act should, in itself, be relevant to an issue before the court – regardless of the statement – therefore the act should not be simply an excuse for admitting the statement.

The statement relates to a contemporaneous physical sensation or mental state

The statement is hearsay if the truth of the statement is at issue: whether in fact the statement's maker did feel ill, for example; it will be admissible hearsay if made contemporaneous with the act such as being poisoned (*R v Horsford* [1898]) or taking out insurance (*Aveson v Lord Kinnaird* [1805]). The statement of physical or mental state must, therefore, be contemporaneous with some act in issue at the trial. In *R v Conde* [1868] a mother was accused of neglect of her child, therefore evidence of the child's complaint of feeling hungry was held to be admissible to demonstrate the neglect.

Circumstantial evidence of a state of mind is not hearsay in the first place, note *Subramaniam v Public Prosecutor* [1956] where the terrorists threats (statements) were not adduced to show that they would in fact carry out the threats (the truth of the threats) but to evidence the victim's state of mind in hearing them. Where the words of the statement are indeed being used to prove the truth of what is stated, a physical or mental state, then the statement will fall to be considered as hearsay. In *R v Gilfoyle* [1996] the court had to consider to what purposes the victim's statements were being put.

❱ R v GILFOYLE [1996]

Basic facts

At his trial for murder the defendant suggested his pregnant wife had committed suicide. A number of suicide notes had been written by his wife, but she had told friends the day after writing them that her husband had asked her to write them for use in a course on suicide at work (he was training to be a nurse). Her demeanour when telling her friends showed concern for why her husband might be asking her to do this, but otherwise she was her usual, happy self.

Relevance

Were the statements admissible to disprove suicidal intent? The Court of Appeal held that the statements were admissible (not hearsay) to prove the fact that they were *made*, and made in a non-suicidal manner. But they would have been hearsay as evidence that she wrote the notes because her husband had asked her to do so and hence to prove her non-suicidal intent. The hearsay exception for proving a contemporaneous state of mind (here a day later was accepted) would, however, allow the statements to be adduced to prove this issue. The court also considered *res gestae* for excited utterances in that the suggestion of writing suicide notes was still dominating the victim's mind the next day.

The usefulness of this exception is limited, because while such statements are admissible as evidence of the sensations, they are inadmissible to prove their cause (*R v Gloster* [1888]). The rule was explained in *R v Nicholas* [1846] as follows:

'If a man says to his surgeon, "I have a pain in the head", or in such a part of the body, that is evidence; but, if he says to his surgeon, "I have a wound"; and was to add "I met John Thomas, who had a sword, and ran me through the body with it", that would be no evidence against John Thomas.'

As regards mental state, an obvious example is a defendant's expression of antipathy towards a murder victim shortly before the latter's death (see Lord Atkinson during argument in *R v Ball* [1911]) or a contemporaneous expressed intention to kill the victim (*R v Moghal* [1977]). An expression of intention to do something has sometimes been relied on to prove that the speaker carried out the act in question. Compare *R v Buckley* [1873] with *R v Wainright* [1875]. In both cases the defendant was charged with murder and in both cases the victim had told the witness of their intention to go to the (respective) defendant's house. While in *Wainright* the statement of intention was not admissible, being only something that might, or might not, have been carried out, in *Buckley* the statement had been admissible. In *Buckley* the victim was a police officer and his intention formed part of his duty to keep his superior officer informed of his whereabouts. Is this the reason why it was admissible: as a police officer's intention is more likely to have been acted upon than the victim's in *Wainright*?

5 CONFESSIONS
At common law, confessions are admissible to prove the matters stated.

6 ADMISSIONS BY AGENTS
Admissions made by an agent acting within the scope of his authority are admissible against his principal. An example of the agent/principal relationship would be a lawyer and his client, such admissions by agents are statements made by the agent to third parties: for example, statements made by counsel in open court and these are admissible as evidence of any matter stated.

7 COMMON ENTERPRISE
Where defendants are charged with conspiracy, or charged jointly with an offence where the prosecution alleges a common enterprise, evidence of acts done or statements made by one defendant in furtherance of the common enterprise will be admissible against those defendants, even though those other defendants were not present at the time when the act was done or the statement made. The reason for this is that a combination of persons for the

purpose of committing a crime is regarded as implying an authority in each to act or speak in furtherance of the common purpose on behalf of the others (*R v Gray* [1995]). There must be independent evidence to prove that the defendant, against whom another's act or statement is to be used, was a member of the common enterprise (*R v Governor of Pentonville Prison ex p Osman* [1990]).

8 EXPERT EVIDENCE

Expert evidence is admissible provided the court requires it in order to make a decision in relation to a specific issue, which falls out of the court's experience or knowledge (*R v Turner* [1975]). Section 127 provides that a statement prepared for the purposes of criminal proceedings by a person who had personal knowledge of the matters stated may be used by another person (the expert) in evidence, provided notice has been given. The expert may thus base an opinion or inference on the statement and, if evidence based on the statement is given, then it is to be treated as evidence of what it states.

SECTION 114(1)(d): ADMISSIBILITY IN THE INTERESTS OF JUSTICE

Section 114(1)(d) contains the new admissibility category of where the admission of the hearsay evidence is required in the interests of justice. In deciding whether a hearsay statement should be admitted under this section, s 114(2) sets out the factors to be considered by the court (as well as any others it considers relevant), such that:

(a) how much probative value the statement has (assuming it to be true) in relation to a matter in issue in the proceedings, or how valuable it is for the understanding of other evidence in the case;

(b) what other evidence has been, or can be, given on the matter or evidence mentioned in paragraph (a);

(c) how important the matter or evidence mentioned in paragraph (a) is in the context of the case as a whole;

(d) the circumstances in which the statement was made;

(e) how reliable the maker of the statement appears to be (*R v Walker* [2007]);

(f) how reliable the evidence of the making of the statement appears to be;

(g) whether oral evidence of the matter stated can be given and, if not, why it cannot;

(h) the amount of difficulty involved in challenging the statement;

(i) the extent to which that difficulty would be likely to prejudice the party facing it.

The factors relate to the weaknesses in hearsay statements and seek a balancing exercise with the accused's Article 6 ECHR right to a fair trial. Whilst the court *must* have regard to all of the above factors, there is no obligation to reach a conclusion on all nine factors. Instead, the court should give consideration to them and others which it considers relevant and assess their significance individually and in relation to each other (*R v Taylor* [2006]). In *R v Z* [2009] the Court of Appeal cautioned against overuse of s 114(1)(d), stating that it 'is to be cautiously applied, since otherwise the conditions laid down by Parliament is s 116 would be cirvumvented'.

The court in *R v Marsh* [2008] suggested that the notion of 'interests of justice' is 'not wholly synonymous with the interests of the Defendant. They mean the public interest in arriving at the right conclusion in the case, including of course the acquittal of anyone whose guilt there is proper doubt.'

In *R v J* [2009] the interests of justice required the admissibility of the hearsay statements by a 30-month-old child ruled incompetent to testify, and in *R v Ladds* [2009] the previous statements of the victim complaining of brutal attacks by his partner. In *R v Khan* [2009], however, the manifest inaccuracies in the witness' account and the fact of her availability pointed clearly to the fact that the witness' hearsay statement should not be adduced, but that she should be called and questioned on her statement.

The 'interests of justice' exception has partially overturned the previous law relating to the admission of a third party's confession. In *R v Blastland* [1986] the court held the third party's confession to be inadmissible hearsay. The judge may now apply the interests of justice test to admit such a hearsay statement (*R v Y* [2008]). But in applying the factors the courts have been slow to admit the statement of an absent witness under s 114(1)(d) when that person could be called to give evidence of the statement. For further details see Chapter 8 on confessions.

The rationale for the inclusion of s 114(1)(d) was to ensure that relevant hearsay evidence is admissible. The discretion for the judge is consistent with developments in other areas of the law, for example the admissibility of sexual behaviour evidence of the complainant to a sexual offence, where the closed-category model of admissibility can cause injustice, and compatible with Article 6 ECHR (*R v Xhabri* [2006]).

PREVIOUS STATEMENTS UNDER SECTIONS 119, 120 AND 139

The Criminal Justice Act 2003 also allows statements fulfilling the criteria for sections 119, 120 and 139 (in certain circumstances) to be adduced for the truth of the matter stated.

OTHER CONSIDERATIONS

Under the Criminal Procedure Rules 2005 a party who wishes to adduce hearsay evidence must give notice to the other party (Rule 34).

MULTIPLE HEARSAY

Section 121 provides that a hearsay statement is not admissible to prove the fact that an earlier hearsay statement has been made, that is, unless either of the statements is admissible under s 117 (business documents), s 119 (inconsistent statements) or s 120 (other previous statements), all the parties to the proceedings agree, *or* the court finds that it is in the interests of justice to admit the later statement.

Thus, unless a hearsay statement falls into either of these three categories, then one hearsay statement may not be relied on to prove, and may not be proved by, another hearsay statement. Generally speaking, therefore, for hearsay falling within ss 116 and 118 the 'interests of justice' test will need to be satisfied before multiple hearsay can be adduced.

CAPABILITY

Section 123 of the Criminal Justice Act 2003 concerns both the capability of the maker of a hearsay statement which is tendered under s 116, 119 or 120 of the 2003 Act and, in the context of a hearsay statement tendered under s 117, the capability of the person who supplied or received information or created or received a document. Section 123 provides that hearsay evidence will not be admitted if the person making or receiving a statement did not have the requisite capability to do so. Under s 114(1)(d) incompetence is not a bar to admissibility, see *R v J* [2009] where having ruled as incompetent a 30-month-old child, the court admitted her hearsay statements implicating her step-father rather than an intruder as the perpetrator of the sexual offence.

CREDIBILITY

Section 124 provides that evidence relevant to the credibility of the maker of the hearsay statement may be admitted in the same manner as if the maker of the statement had given direct oral evidence. This provision allows the cross-examining party to challenge the credibility of a statement's maker as though the witness were present, thus if the witness has a reputation for untruthfulness, for example, this may be revealed.

UNCONVINCING EVIDENCE

Where a case against a defendant is wholly or partly based upon a hearsay statement and such evidence proves to be so unconvincing that any conviction based on it would be unsafe, s 125 allows a court to stop a trial by jury at any time after the close of the case by the prosecution. In such circumstances, the court must direct the jury to acquit the defendant of the offence, order a retrial or discharge the jury.

GENERAL DISCRETION TO EXCLUDE

Section 126 provides that a court may refuse to admit hearsay evidence if the court is satisfied that the case for excluding it, taking account of the danger that to admit it would result in undue waste of time, substantially outweighs the case for admitting it, taking into account the value of the evidence. See *R v Joyce and another* [2005] where it was held that hearsay evidence consisting of previous inconsistent statements was appropriately admitted, despite the witnesses wishing to retract their earlier statements on the basis of mistaken identification. It was in reality a case of intimidation.

SECTION 78 DISCRETION TO EXCLUDE

In addition to the s 126 discretion, s 78 of the Police and Criminal Evidence Act 1984 (PACE) provides:

1   In any proceedings the court may refuse to allow evidence on which the prosecution proposes to rely to be given if it appears to the court that, having regard to all the circumstances, including the circumstances in which the evidence was obtained, the admission of the evidence would have such an adverse effect on the fairness of the proceedings that the court ought not to admit it.

THE CIVIL EVIDENCE ACT 1995

By s 1(1) of the Act, in civil proceedings, evidence shall not be excluded on the ground that it is hearsay. Multiple hearsay, as well as first-hand hearsay, is admissible.

Sections 2–4 provide safeguards in relation to hearsay evidence. There is a general duty on parties under s 2(1) to give warning of the intention to adduce hearsay evidence. But by s 2(4) failure to comply with this duty is not to affect the admissibility of the evidence. Section 3 provides a power to call for cross-examination a person whose statement has been tendered as hearsay evidence. Statutory guidelines for weighing hearsay evidence are provided in s 4.

Sections 5–7 are supplementary provisions. The maker of a statement adduced as hearsay evidence must have been competent to give direct oral evidence at the time that the statement was made. There are provisions to admit evidence to attack or support the credibility of the maker of a hearsay statement, as well as evidence to show that the maker of the statement made inconsistent statements, either before or after the statement was made.

By s 8, where a statement contained in a document is admissible as evidence in civil proceedings, it can be proved by the production of the original document or a copy authenticated in such a manner as the court shall approve. It is immaterial how many levels of copying have taken place between the original and the copy.

Section 9 concerns the proof of records of a business or public authority. Its effect is that documents, including those stored by a computer, forming part of such records are admissible as hearsay evidence under s 1, and the ordinary notice provisions apply. Unless the court otherwise directs, a document shall be taken to form part of the records of a business or public authority if there is produced to the court a certificate to that effect signed by an officer of the business or authority. The absence of an entry in such records may be proved by affidavit of an officer of the business or authority in question.

You should now be confident that you would be able to tick all of the boxes on the checklist at the beginning of this chapter. To check your knowledge of Hearsay why not visit the companion website and take the Multiple Choice Question test. Check your understanding of the terms and vocabulary used in this chapter with the flashcard glossary.

8

Confessions

Although confessions are out of court statements adduced to prove the truth of their contents, they are admissible as an exception to the hearsay rule under s 76(1) of the Police and Criminal Evidence Act 1984 (PACE). It is recognised, however, that considerations of fairness or reliability may make it undesirable to admit evidence of a particular confession or of some other item of prosecution evidence. Sections 76 and 78 of PACE deal respectively with confessions and with a discretion to exclude, for reasons of fairness, evidence on which the prosecution proposes to rely. To try to secure reliability and fairness, Codes of Practice have been created under ss 60(1)(a) and 66 of PACE. The Codes attempt to control the ways in which certain types of evidence are obtained and breaches may lead to exclusion of an item of evidence under s 76 or s 78. The sections are often relied on in the alternative; in *R v Mason* [1988], it was held that s 78 applies to confessions as much as to any other kind of prosecution evidence.

By s 76(2), if in any proceedings:

- the prosecution proposes to give in evidence a confession made by an accused person; and

- it is represented to the court that the confession was or may have been obtained:

    (a) by oppression of the person who made it; or
    (b) in consequence of anything said or done which was likely, in the circumstances existing at the time, to render unreliable any confession which might be made by him in consequence thereof,

the court shall not allow the confession to be given in evidence *unless* the prosecution can prove that the confession (notwithstanding that it may be true) was *not* obtained in the circumstances referred to in (a) or (b) of the subsection.

By sub-s (3), the court may of its own motion require the prosecution to satisfy it that a confession was not obtained in either of these circumstances.

By sub-s (4), the fact that a confession is wholly or partly excluded under sub-s (2) shall not affect the admissibility in evidence of any facts discovered as a result of the confession. By the same sub-section, where a confession has a relevance that goes beyond the truth of its contents, because it shows that the defendant speaks, writes or expresses himself in a particular way, so much of the confession as is necessary to show that he does so will be admissible.

According to s 118(1)5 of the Criminal Justice Act 2003 the rules relating to the admissibility of confession evidence or mixed statements are preserved.

RECOGNISING A CONFESSION

By s 82(1) of PACE, 'confession' includes any statement wholly or partly adverse to the person who made it, whether made to a person in authority or not, and whether made in words or otherwise. An apparently wholly exculpatory statement does not amount to a confession if it becomes adverse to its maker because it appears to be evasive or because it is subsequently discovered to be false (*R v Sat-Bhambra* [1989], *R v Hasan* [2005]).

The partial definition in PACE assumes that a statement can be made by non-verbal means and there are cases that suggest that an admission can be made by conduct. In *Moriarty v London, Chatham and Dover Rly Co* [1870], a plaintiff's attempts to persuade several persons to give false evidence in support of his claim were held to be evidence of an admission by conduct that the case he was putting forward was untrue. Even silence alone may amount to a confession if it can be construed as an adoption of an accusation by the person against whom it is made. The circumstances must be that the persons are on equal terms, the person remained silent when an accusation was made, and the circumstances were such that remaining silent could be inferred as an acceptance of the accusation. And so answers to a police officer will not usually fulfil the requirements (*Parkes v R* [1976]). Also, in *R v Batt* [1995], the failure of one defendant to dissociate himself from incriminating observations made by his companion was held to amount to evidence against him.

EXCLUDING A CONFESSION UNDER SECTION 76 OF PACE

OPPRESSION

Section 76(2)(a) provides for exclusion where the confession was, or may have been, obtained by oppression.

By s 76(8), oppression includes torture, inhuman or degrading treatment and the use or threat of violence (whether or not amounting to torture). This is an inclusive, rather than an exclusive, definition. Further guidance can be obtained from *R v Fulling* [1987], in which Lord Lane said that the word should be given its ordinary dictionary meaning, namely:

> Exercise of authority or power in a burdensome, harsh or wrongful manner; unjust or cruel treatment of subjects, inferiors, etc; the imposition of unreasonable or unjust burdens.

This quotation should not however be read as if it were itself a statutory definition; the context makes it clear that Lord Lane was emphasising the seriousness of the conduct envisaged. Physical violence, however, or the threat of it, are not essential elements. In *R v Paris, Abdullahi and Miller* [1993], it was held that interviews had been oppressive where a suspect had been verbally bullied.

▶ **R v PARIS, ABDULLAHI AND MILLER [1993]**

Basic facts

This is the (in)famous case of the 'Cardiff Three' who were subjected to horrific treatment by the South Wales police in relation to an investigation for murder. The defendants were accused of the murder of a prostitute Lynette White who was stabbed some 50 times. After a trial in which the prosecution relied on the evidence of two discredited witnesses and admissions made by Miller after exhaustive interviews all three were convicted. Miller was described by a defence doctor as 'on the borderline of mental handicap with an IQ of 75, a mental age of 11 and a reading age of 8'. The officers shouted at one suspect and told him what they wanted him to say despite his denying involvement some 300 times.

Relevance

This case has overall importance in the area of improperly obtained confessions and how they can be excluded. The Court of Appeal in this case, whose members had not heard an actual interrogation before, was appalled by what they heard and had no hesitation in finding that it was oppressive within s 76(2)(a).

▶ R v FULLING [1987]

Basic facts

The defendant was convicted of obtaining property by deception. During the interview she claimed that the detective told her that her boyfriend had been having an affair with someone who was in the cell next to her. She argued that this amounted to oppression and her confession, therefore, should be excluded.

Relevance

This case gave a definition of what oppression is; that it is 'something above and beyond that which is inherently oppressive on police custody' and is therefore a useful marker in determining what might amount to oppression. The oppressive nature of being in a police station will not be satisfactory.

The statute excludes a confession which was or may have been *obtained by* oppression. It therefore remains theoretically possible that there could be an instance of oppression that does not in fact cause a particular confession to be made. In those circumstances, the sub-section would not be available to the defence.

CIRCUMSTANCES SUGGESTING UNRELIABILITY

By s 76(2)(b), a confession will be excluded where it was, or may have been, obtained in consequence of anything said or done which was likely, in the circumstances existing at the time, to render unreliable any confession which might be made by the defendant in consequence thereof. The test is, therefore, one of *hypothetical* rather than *actual* reliability (see *R v Cox* [1991]).

With s 76(2)(b), as with s 76(2)(a), a causative link between the matters complained of and a confession must be shown, at least as a possibility, before there can be exclusion. The usual approach to s 76(2)(b) has been to say that 'anything said or done' had to refer to something said or done by some person other than the suspect (see, for example, *R v Goldenberg* [1989]). Once an external factor making for unreliability could be shown, it is then open to the court to take into account the personal circumstances of the person making the confession, because they are part of the 'circumstances existing at the time' which, by s 76(2)(b), are to be taken into account when considering reliability (see, for example, *R v McGovern* [1993]).

Section 78 PACE is also relevant to exclude confessions on which the prosecution proposes to rely, where admission would 'have such an adverse effect on the fairness of proceedings that the court ought not to admit it'. Consequently, confessions obtained after breach of a suspect's right to legal advice have very often been excluded. The right, which is set out in s 58 of PACE, is regarded as 'one of the most important and fundamental rights of a citizen' (*R v Samuel* [1988]). In *R v Samuel* [1988] the defendant was wrongly refused access to a solicitor, allegedly on the basis that the police believed that *any* solicitor he spoke to *might* unwittingly pass on information to others being sought in connection with the offence. The court held in this case that the breaches of the Code were flagrant and excluded the confession under s 78. Similarly, in *R v Absolam* [1988] a confession was excluded after the custody officer questioned the defendant without warning him about his right to legal advice and without making a contemporary record of the interview. The case of *R v Alladice* [1988], on the other hand, was decided on its own exceptional facts which included an admission by the defendant on the *voir dire* that he was well able to cope with police interviews and had asked for a solicitor only to have a check on police conduct.

Where a defendant has made an admission that is vulnerable to s 76 or s 78 at a first interview, a similar admission at a later interview may also be capable of being inadmissible, even though the original vitiating elements are no longer present, because the very fact of having made an earlier admission is likely to have an effect on the later interview (*R v Canale* [1990]). The question however, is one of fact and degree and is likely to depend on whether the objections leading to the exclusion of the first interview were of a fundamental and continuing nature and, if so, whether the arrangements for the subsequent interview gave the defendant a sufficient opportunity to exercise an informed and independent choice as to whether he should repeat or retract what he said in the first interview or say nothing (*R v Neil* [1994]; *R v Nelson and Rose* [1998]; *R v Owusu* [2007]).

THE PROCEDURE

It is a matter of law (and so a question for the judge) whether a confession is admissible. The judge will determine admissibility in the absence of the jury on a *voir dire*. But once the judge rules a confession admissible, and the defendant suggests grounds for inadmissibility, the jury will ultimately decide if they believe that it was not obtained in the two prohibited ways and the weight to attach to it. Consequently, while the judge may hold there was insufficient evidence of oppression or unreliability, and so allow admissibility, the jury may use the same 'inadequate' evidence to deem an admissible confession to have little weight or if the jury do decide that the confession should be inadmissible they will be told to disregard it in their evidence even if they believe it to be true.

In English law an accused can be convicted solely on the evidence of a confession; according to *R v Baldry* [1852] a confession is the best evidence available.

Once the confession is deemed inadmissible under either provision there is no residual discretion to allow the evidence on the behalf of the prosecution; there is the possibility of admitting on the behalf of a co-accused under s 76A.

Section 76

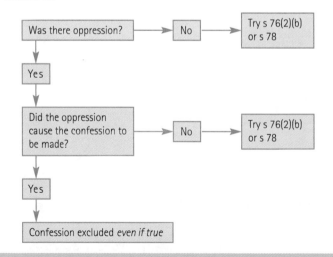

Note it would appear to be the case that a confession is not admissible under the s 114(1)(d) inclusionary discretion, due to s 128(2) CJA 2003, which is to the effect that confessions are governed by s 76 PACE only: 'nothing in this chapter makes a confession by a defendant admissible if it would not be admissible under s 76 PACE'.

USE OF CONFESSIONS BY A CO-DEFENDANT

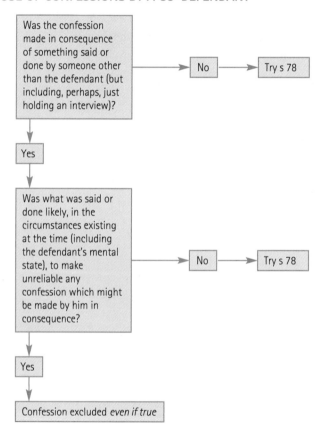

What one defendant says outside court when not in the presence of a co-accused will be evidence against the speaker, but not against the co-accused (*R v Gunewardene* [1951]), but such a statement will not automatically be 'edited' at trial so as to exclude the parts that are inadmissible against a co-accused. The judge has a discretionary power to exclude relevant evidence on which the *prosecution* proposes to rely so as to ensure a fair trial, but this does not extend to the exculpatory part of a mixed statement on which a *defendant* proposes to rely, for example, in which he has put the blame on another defendant (*R v Lobban* [1995]).

Note, however, that what one defendant says *when giving evidence in court* is evidence against a co-defendant whom it implicates (*R v Rudd* [1948]). In *R v Johnson* [2007] the Court of Appeal ruled that a guilty plea and the written basis of plea, for the purposes of s 76A of PACE, amounted to a confession and it was admissible when the co-accused requested it to be so under s 76A(1) of PACE. Note a defendant under s 76A can seek to admit a confession made by the co-defendant charged in the same proceedings, provided it is *relevant* to a matter in issue. The confession can be excluded on the same bases found under s 76 for the prosecution, but the standard of proof for the defendant is the balance of probabilities (s 76A(2)). Section 76A(3) further provides that the court may of its own accord decide that before admitting such evidence it needs to be proven on a balance of probabilities that the confession was not obtained in this manner.

▶ R v JOHNSON [2007]

Basic facts

Two defendants pleaded not guilty to a charge of importing drugs. One defendant had, however, originally admitted the offence and entered a guilty plea at an earlier stage in the proceedings. He had then made a successful application to 'vacate the guilty plea', and so pleaded not guilty at trial.

Relevance

The earlier admission and guilty plea was still on record and admissible by the co-defendant. The trial judge had no discretion to refuse the admission of the confession.

CONFESSIONS OF THIRD PARTIES NOT CHARGED IN THE PROCEEDINGS

Section 76 PACE only concerns the admissilbity of confessions of persons charged in the same proceedings. Where the defendant seeks to admit the confession of a third party (who is not charged in the same proceedings) admissibility may be secured by using the s 114(1)(d) 'interests of justice' test for hearsay. Of course the maker of the confession could also be called as a witness.

The previous position was that in *R v Blastland* [1986] where a third party confessed to the crime. Blastland was not allowed to refer to the third party's confession to exculpate him and similarly under the old law a confession by a non-defendant could not be admitted by the prosecution if the person had implicated the defendant. Now s 114(1)(d) allows the admittance of the third party's confession if the 'interests of justice' test is satisfied (*R v Y* [2008]).

In *R v Finch* [2007] F and R were charged with possession of a prohibited firearm as they were both in the car when it was stopped by police and both their fingerprints were on the bag containing the gun. R pleaded guilty and in his police statement suggested that F had had nothing to do with it. Instead, it was suggested, the presence of F's fingerprint was by innocent touching of the bag. Consequently, the defendant (F) wanted to adduce R's (third party) statement at his trial. The court refused to admit R's statement under s 114(1)(d) in the interests of justice, suggesting that R could have been called by F to give evidence at trial and restate his words in court on oath, and if he denied it then it could have been put to him as a previous inconsistent statement and proved if necessary.

There is also the chance that the judge would allow admissibility of a third party's statement under s 116 as hearsay from an absent witness, if he has since absconded or is 'in fear' of giving evidence.

FACTS DISCOVERED AS A RESULT OF THE CONFESSION

Section 76A(4) provides that if a confession is wholly or partly excluded, then this will not affect the admissibility of evidence of any facts discovered as a result of the confession, or where the confession is relevant as showing that the accused speaks, writes or expresses himself in a particular way, of so much of the confession as is necessary to show that he does so. Consequently, the so-called 'fruit of the poisoned tree' is admissible; the fruit being a fact such as the location of the murder weapon discovered as a result of an unlawful confession. The basis for admissibility of the fact is based on reliability, while the confession may be inadmissible on public policy grounds if oppression was used, for example, the fact discovered as a result would be reliable.

In *A v Secretary of State for the Home Department (No 2)* [2005] the House of Lords upheld the UK position as regards real evidence found as a result of an inadmissible confession, such that 'there is an obvious anomaly in treating an involuntary statement as inadmissible while treating as admissible evidence which would never have come to light but for the involuntary statement. But this is an anomaly which the English common law has accepted, no doubt regarding it as a pragmatic compromise between the rejection of the involuntary statement and the practical desirability of relying on probative evidence which can be adduced without the need to rely on the involuntary statement.'

You should now be confident that you would be able to tick all of the boxes on the checklist at the beginning of this chapter. To check your knowledge of Confessions why not visit the companion website and take the Multiple Choice Question test. Check your understanding of the terms and vocabulary used in this chapter with the flashcard glossary.

9

Character evidence

For evidential purposes, the term 'character' can refer to a person's general reputation; their general disposition to behave in a particular way or to specific examples of misconduct, such as previous convictions. Character can be relevant to the credibility of a witness or, in the case of the defendant, the issue of whether he is guilty or not. Character evidence can be of both good character and bad character. There are special considerations, and hence special rules, governing character evidence of the defendant. The Criminal Justice Act 2003 introduced a new statutory regime to govern the admissibility of bad character of all witnesses, abolishing the common law rules in this area; the common law rules governing the admissibility of good character evidence of the defendant remains.

GOOD CHARACTER

GOOD CHARACTER OF NON-DEFENDANTS

Generally speaking the party calling the witness will try to elicit good character traits of the witness, by suggesting that he is a family man, has a professional job or steady job, or is a religious person. A party is not allowed, however, to directly suggest that the witness is of good character (other than defendants).

GOOD CHARACTER OF THE DEFENDANT

The common law rules governing the admission of evidence of good character are preserved by ss 99(2) and 118(1) of the Criminal Justice Act 2003, which provides for the continuation of 'any rule of law under which in criminal proceedings evidence of reputation is admissible for the purpose of proving good character, but only so far as it allows the court to treat such evidence as proving the matter concerned'.

EVIDENCE OF GOOD CHARACTER IN CRIMINAL PROCEEDINGS

There are limitations on the sort of evidence that can be adduced for the purpose of showing that a defendant, because of his good character, is unlikely to be guilty. Under the rule in *R v Rowton* [1865], only evidence of general reputation is admissible as evidence of good character. While the Rowton principle includes the fact that the defendant has no previous convictions, evidence of the opinions of specific persons and evidence of specific good acts performed by the defendant are inadmissible. In practice, however, judges do not always keep strictly to these rules, but it is clear from *R v Redgrave* [1981] that any relaxation of the rule is an indulgence by the court and not a defendant's right.

THE SIGNIFICANCE OF GOOD CHARACTER

Where evidence of good character is given, its significance must be explained to the jury. Any judicial direction is now governed by rules laid down by the Court of Appeal in *R v Vye* [1993] (and is often referred to as a '*Vye* direction'). This case recognised two 'limbs' about good character:

■ the relevance of good character to credibility;

■ the relevance of good character to the question of guilt or innocence ('propensity').

The *Vye* direction must be given not only where the defendant gives evidence of his good character, or calls a character witness to do the same, but also where he relies in support of his defence on exculpatory statements made to police or others. Because good character is relevant to credibility, the judge should tell the jury to have regard to the defendant's good character when considering the credibility of those statements.

In addition, the court in *R v Gray* [2004] set out the following principles to deal with various problem cases:

1   The primary rule is that a person of previous good character must be given a full direction covering both credibility and propensity. Where there are no further facts to complicate the position, such a direction is mandatory and should be unqualified (*Vye*, *R v Aziz* [1996]).

2   If a defendant has a previous conviction which, either because of its age or its nature, may entitle him to be treated as of effective good character, the trial judge has a discretion so to treat him, and if he does so the defendant is entitled to a *Vye* direction (passim); but

3   Where the previous conviction can only be regarded as irrelevant or of no significance in relation to the offence charged, that discretion ought to be exercised in favour of treating the defendant as of good character. In such a case the defendant is again entitled to a *Vye* direction. It would seem to be consistent with principle (4) below that, where there is room for uncertainty as to how a defendant of effective good character should be

treated, a judge would be entitled to give an appropriately modified *Vye* direction.

4   Where a defendant of previous good character, whether absolute or, we would suggest, effective, has been shown at trial, whether by admission or otherwise, to be guilty of criminal conduct, the prima facie rule of practice is to deal with this by qualifying a *Vye* direction rather than by withholding it; but

5   In such a case, there remains a narrowly circumscribed residual discretion to withhold a good character direction in whole, or presumably in part, where it would make no sense, or would be meaningless or absurd or an insult to common sense, to do otherwise.

6   Approved examples of the exercise of such a residual discretion are not common. Lord Steyn in *Aziz* appears to have considered that a person of previous good character who is shown beyond doubt to have been guilty of serious criminal behaviour similar to the offence charged would forfeit his right to any direction.

7   A direction should never be misleading. Where therefore a defendant has withheld something of his record so that otherwise a trial judge is not in a position to refer to it, the defendant may forfeit the more ample, if qualified, direction which the judge might have been able to give.

▶ R v VYE [1993]

Basic facts

The two defendants were charged with conspiracy to evade the payment of VAT. While neither had criminal convictions they admitted, during the trial, to other acts of dishonesty. Entitlement to a good character direction arose.

Relevance

The House of Lords held that they continued to be entitled to both limbs of the good character direction, but because it would be wrong to mislead the jury, the judge should add some qualification by reference to the conduct admitted by the accused. Ultimately, it was added, the judge has discretion to withhold either or both limbs of the direction where the accused's claim to a good character is 'spurious'.

Failure to give a *Vye* direction where it is appropriate can lead to the quashing of a conviction (*R v Fulcher* [1995]). As can be seen from principle 4 from *Gray*, in giving the direction, a judge is entitled to take into account the fact that, although without previous convictions, a defendant had previously been the subject of a formal police caution in respect of another offence. (This is not to be confused with the caution given to persons suspected of offences after arrest or before interview.) Since a pre-condition of administering this type of caution is an admission of guilt by the person cautioned, a judge may decide to direct the jury as to the relevance of the defendant's lack of previous convictions in relation to his credibility, but not to give the second limb of the direction in relation to propensity (*R v Martin* [1999]).

Doubtful cases of good character
Sometimes, a defendant will admit, as part of his defence, to *some* wrongdoing, though not that alleged by the prosecution. If he has no previous convictions, the *Vye* directions should usually still be given, subject to whatever qualification the judge thinks appropriate (*R v Aziz* [1996]). When a defendant has already pleaded guilty to some counts on an indictment, but is contesting others, the earlier pleas will generally mean that he is no longer of good character. Any direction about character in such a case will be a matter for the judge's discretion (*R v Challenger* [1994]).

Spent convictions and good character
With the leave of the judge, a defendant with spent convictions can be presented as a person of good character, provided the jury is not misled (*R v Bailey* [1989]). He can therefore be described as, for example, 'a man of good character with no relevant convictions'. Even if a conviction is not spent, it may be similarly overlooked if it is minor and of no significance in the context of the current charge (*R v H* [1994]; *R v Payton* [2006]). If an earlier conviction is ignored or, though mentioned, treated as irrelevant, the judge should give the *Vye* direction (*R v H* [1994]).

BAD CHARACTER

Bad character evidence is dealt with in Part 11 of the Criminal Justice Act 2003 (CJA) which came into force on the 15 December 2004 and applies to all trials and Newton hearings which began on or after the 15 December 2004 (*R v Bradley* [2005]).

DEFINITION OF BAD CHARACTER – SECTION 98 OF THE CJA 2003

This definition applies to both defendants and non-defendants and provides that any reference to 'bad character' refers to evidence of, or of a disposition towards, misconduct on his part, other than evidence which has to do with the alleged facts of the offence with which the defendant is charged, or is evidence of misconduct in connection with the investigation or prosecution of that offence.

The reference to 'evidence which has to do with the alleged facts of the offence with which the defendant is charged', excludes from the bad character provisions any misconduct during the alleged offence, or its investigation (for example providing a false alibi). The phrase 'to do with' has been defined to refer to 'some nexus in time' or contemporaneity between the offence with which the defendant was charged and the misconduct or 'so closely connected with those alleged facts' (*R v Tirnaneanu* [2007] and *R v Machado* [2006]). In *Machado* the time nexus was satisfied with evidence that the victim had taken an ecstasy tablet shortly before the alleged robbery, with the inference that the victim was not robbed but simply fell over. Similarly, matters immediately following the commission of the offence could be 'to do with the offence' (*R v McIntosh* [2006]), as can acts by way of preparation for the offence or acts upon which the later offence are based. In *R v O'Connor* [2009] events both leading up to the assault and after it were 'to do with' the offence in showing the defendant's mindset at the time. In *Tirnaneanu*, on the other hand, the misconduct involved other separate occasions when the defendant had falsely represented himself as a solicitor for illegal immigrants and was not found to be sufficiently 'to do with' the charged incident, thus falling to be considered as evidence of 'bad character' under s 98 (see also *R v Saleem* [2007]).

▶ R v SALEEM [2007]

Basic facts

The assault took place on the defendant's birthday, when he and others were alleged to have committed causing grievous bodily harm with intent. The defendant had violent images and rap lyrics on his computer, and had accessed them a few days before the offence. Rap lyrics created months before the assault, had been altered significantly by the defendant and accessed ten days before it; they read 'my birth day im gon make it ur worst day'.

Relevance

The court held that the rap lyrics were not admissible as having 'to do with the facts of the offence' due to insufficient connection in time with the facts of the offence. Nor were they evidence of a motive or reason for committing the offence. They thus fell to be considered as bad character under s 98 and were admitted to disprove 'innocent presence' at the scene.

SECTION 112(1) OF THE CJA 2003

Section 112(1) defines 'misconduct' as 'the commission of an offence or other reprehensible behaviour' (*R v Manister* [2005] and *R v Hong Quang* [2005]). The definition is broad and will incorporate: evidence of previous convictions; evidence of other charges being tried concurrently; evidence of previous charges not pursued by the prosecution and acquittals (*R v Edwards (Stewart) and Others* [2006]). Nevertheless, it is certainly not the case that the courts will always allow criminal allegations that have not resulted in convictions to be adduced. Each case will turn on its own facts, and it is likely that judges will heed the warning given by Rose LJ in *R v Hanson, Gilmore and Pickering* [2005] that: 'Where past events are disputed the judge must take care not to permit the trial unreasonably to be diverted into an investigation of matters not charged on the indictment' (see *R v O'Dowd* [2009]). So-called satellite trials might be necessary where an unproven allegation, or even an allegation that the defendant was tried and acquitted for, is to be relied upon as bad character evidence where the judge sees it as being sufficiently relevant (*R v Lowe* [2007]). In *Lowe*, *R v Ngyuen* [2008] and *R v McKensie* [2008] the Court of Appeal established that the jury would need to be satisfied beyond reasonable doubt that the defendant committed that misconduct before they could use it as bad character evidence against him. In *Ngyuen* the defendant was charged with murder, by glassing the victim, but the prosecution deliberately chose not to charge him with a separate offence (also involving the defendant using a glass as a weapon) alleged two weeks earlier, using the incident instead as bad character evidence to demonstrate his propensity for violence.

In essence, charges which have resulted in an acquittal will generally only be relevant where the modus operandi or surrounding facts are similar so as to make a link between the acquitted charges and those currently on trial. So for example in *R v Z* [2000] rape allegations which were the subject of an earlier acquittal were used to show the similarity with how the defendant had endeared himself to each complainant, took them out on a date and then turned violent and raped them when his advances were spurned (see also *R v Boulton* [2007]).

Reprehensible behaviour is not defined by statute but it will not include behaviour of which the court does not condone (*R v Gary Osbourne* [2007]). Meanwhile recent cases have confirmed the following as not demonstrating reprehensible behaviour: the legal possession of an antique, but functional, firearm (*R v McLean* [2006]), an overdose (by a witness) (*R v Hall-Chung* [2007]), psychiatric illness (*R v Gary Osbourne* [2007]) and lawful sexual relationship with an adult female despite a large age gap (*R v Manister* [2005]). In *R v Weir* [2005], however, evidence from two women alleging sexually charged approaches and manipulation by their Hindu priest, at a vulnerable time in their lives, was deemed reprehensible even though these had not resulted in any crimes. Similarly the previous case of *R v Marsh* [1994] would appear consistent with post-CJA case law, causing the defendant's poor disciplinary record for violence on the rugby field to be reprehensible behaviour.

Disposition concerns a tendency, propensity or an inclination for a person to behave in a particular way.

MORE THAN ONE OFFENCE ON THE INDICTMENT

Section 112(2) provides that where a defendant is charged with two or more offences in the same proceedings, each offence on the indictment is treated as if it was charged in separate proceedings. The effect of this is that if the prosecution wish to adduce evidence of the alleged facts of one offence with which the defendant is charged then this will be treated as bad character evidence for the purposes of admissibility in relation to one or more of the other offences with which he is charged on the indictment. Consequently, the bad character evidence must be admissible through one of the seven 'gateways' listed in s 101.

PERSONS OTHER THAN THE DEFENDANT: NON-DEFENDANT'S BAD CHARACTER

The bad character evidence of the non-defendant is governed by s 100 of the CJA 2003. Non-defendants are not actually defined in the Act but include victims, whether or not they give evidence, witnesses and third parties who are not witnesses in the case. Remember that generally the credibility of a witness is viewed as a collateral matter and is subject to rule on finality of answers. The rationale behind the strict rules of admissibility in the CJA 2003 for adducing evidence of the bad character of non-defendant witnesses was to protect witnesses from gratuitous attack by the defendant. One element of the strict approach to admissibility is the requirement of leave.

LEAVE OF THE COURT

Unless evidence is being adduced under s 101(1)(c) (all the parties to the proceedings agree to the evidence being admissible), evidence of the bad character of a person other than the defendant must not be given without leave of the court. In deciding whether to grant leave, the court must have regard to sections 100(1)–(3).

Section 100(1) provides that for bad character of a person other than the defendant to be admissible it must either be:

(a) important explanatory evidence, or

(b) of substantial *probative value* in relation to a matter which:
    (i) is a matter in issue in the proceedings, and
    (ii) is of substantial importance in the context of the case as a whole.

IMPORTANT EXPLANATORY EVIDENCE

This is essentially background evidence and s 100(2) provides that without such evidence, the court or jury would find it impossible or difficult to properly understand the other evidence in the case, and its value for understanding the case as a whole is substantial.

SUBSTANTIAL PROBATIVE VALUE

Section 100(3) provides that when the court is assessing the probative value of evidence, it must have regard to the nature and number of the events, or other things, to which the evidence relates and to when those events or things are alleged to have happened or existed (*R v Yaxlev-Lennon* [2005]). Where evidence is evidence of misconduct the court must consider the nature and extent of the similarities and the dissimilarities between each of the alleged instances of misconduct and the extent to which the evidence shows or tends to show that the same person was responsible each time. The court may also consider other factors which it feels are relevant.

A DEFENDANT'S BAD CHARACTER

Leave to adduce evidence of a defendant's bad character is not required. This is in contrast to the non-defendant (previously discussed) where, unless all parties agreed, leave to adduce such evidence is required by the court. Instead, if the prosecution intend to adduce evidence of a defendant's (or co-defendant's bad character) they should serve notice to the defence (s 111(2)) indicating the nature of the bad character evidence and the prescribed 'gateway' under s 101(1) through which they intend to adduce the evidence. In *R v Campbell* [2007] the Court of Appeal ruled that when evidence of bad character is introduced, the jury should be assisted in its relevance and giving them the Judicial Studies Board specimen directions with no other guidance was not acceptable. Where, however, the jury is not given adequate help this does not automatically render a conviction unsafe (*R v Saleem* [2007]).

THE SEVEN GATEWAYS

Although this is the method through which evidence of bad character is adduced, in *R v Wallace* [2007] the Court of Appeal ruled that the important issue was not the defendant's propensity to be untruthful or to commit offences but looking at the circumstantial evidence and deciding whether this pointed to him committing each offence with which he was charged.

Under s 101(1) evidence of the defendant's bad character in criminal proceedings is *only* admissible if:

1 All the parties to the proceedings agree to the evidence being admissible (s 101(1)(a))

This section accommodates for the situation where all parties agree that the evidence should be admitted.

2 The evidence is adduced by the defendant himself or is given in answer to a question asked by him in cross-examination and intended to elicit it (s 101(1)(b))

A defendant may choose to admit such evidence himself during examination-in-chief in an attempt to persuade a jury to look upon him more favourably and possibly as someone with nothing to hide. Similarly a defendant might feel that adducing his bad character might be helpful to his case, for example, where a defendant raises an alibi and that alibi involves evidence of bad character in some way, or where it is likely that his convictions will be admissible anyway.

3 It is important explanatory evidence (s 101(1)(c))

Section 102 defines 'important explanatory evidence' as evidence, without which, the court or jury would find it impossible or difficult properly to understand other evidence in the case and its value for understanding the case as a whole is substantial. This is the same definition as important explanatory evidence in s 100(2) when dealing with a non-defendant's bad character. If the evidence is more than minor or more than trivial it will be admissible if it assists the court to understand the case as a whole.

The courts need to be vigilant in ensuring that evidence which is really concerned with propensity is not adduced under s 101(1)(c) in the guise of explanatory evidence (*R v Ifzal Iqbal* [2006] where the prosecution sought to adduce the defendant's previous drug convictions to demonstrate non-innocent touching of the bags containing drugs).

In *R v Edwards (Karl) and others* [2006] explanatory bad character evidence (the fact the defendant had been the witness' drug dealer) was admissible to support the correctness of her identification of him which was central to the case. Similarly, in *R v Bourgass* [2005] the prosecution adduced evidence to show the real circumstances in which the defendant attempted to flee from the police and killed an officer were that his premises had been recently raided and found to contain explosives and toxic chemicals (ricin and cyanide) to be used for terrorism. See also *R v Sawoniuk* [2000].

4 It is relevant to an important matter in issue between the defendant and his prosecution (s 101(1)(d))

Section 101(1)(d) allows for bad character evidence where 'it is relevant to an important matter in issue between the defence and prosecution' and so includes bad character that negatives coincidence or innocent presence at the scene (*R v Saleem* [2007]) or innocent association (*R v Jordan* [2009]), as well as the issue of propensity. Section 103(1) provides matters in issue between the defendant and the prosecution include the question whether the defendant has a propensity to commit offences of the kind with which he is charged, except where his having such a propensity makes it no more likely that he is guilty of the offence. Similarly it includes the question whether the defendant has a propensity to be untruthful, except where it is not suggested that the defendant's case is untruthful in any respect.

Definition of propensity

Section 103(2) suggests that, apart from any other means, a defendant's propensity to commit offences of the kind with which he is charged may be established by evidence that he has been convicted of:

(a) an offence of the same description as the one with which he is charged, or

(b) an offence of the same category as the one with which he is charged.

Offences of the same 'description' refers to a particular law that has been broken, rather than the circumstances in which it was committed. Currently to date only two such 'categories of offences' have been prescribed, namely the 'theft category' (Criminal Justice Act 2003 (Categories of Offences) Order 2004 (SI 2004/3346)) and the 'sexual offences category' (persons under the age of 16) (Criminal Justice Act 2003 (Categories of Offences) Order 2004 (SI 2004/3346)).

Propensity to commit offences

Section 103(2) makes clear that this does not prevent the admission of convictions which are neither of the same description nor the same category from being relied upon as evidence of a defendant's propensity to commit offences of the *kind* which he is charged. The test is not simply whether the defendant has committed the offence(s) in question but rather whether he has a (presumably current) propensity to commit such offences (*R v Hanson, Gilmore,*

Pickstone [2005]). The Court of Appeal in Hanson laid down guidance for courts in considering admissibility under s 101(1)(d), such that:

▨ There is no minimum number of events necessary to demonstrate such a propensity.

▨ The fewer the number of convictions the weaker is likely to be the evidence of propensity.

▨ A single previous conviction for an offence of the same description or category will often not show propensity. But it may do so where, for example, it shows a tendency to unusual behaviour or where its circumstances (eg modus operandi) demonstrate probative force in relation to the offence charged. Child sexual abuse or fire setting are comparatively clear examples of such unusual behaviour (*R v Pickering* [2005]).

▨ It will often be necessary, before determining admissibility to examine each individual conviction rather than merely to look at the name of the offence or at the defendant's record as a whole (see *R v Beverley* [2006]).

▨ The sentence passed will not normally be probative or admissible at the behest of the Crown, though it may be at the behest of the defence.

▨ Where past events are disputed the Judge must take care not to permit the trial unreasonably to be diverted into an investigation of matters not charged on the indictment.

Where propensity to commit the offence is relied upon, *Hanson* established that, there are thus essentially three questions to be considered (paragraph 7):

1 Does the history of conviction(s) establish a propensity to commit offences of the kind charged?
2 Does that propensity make it more likely that the defendant committed the offence charged?
3 Is it unjust to rely on the conviction(s) of the same description or category; and, in any event, will the proceedings be unfair if they are admitted (s 101(3))?

The court needs to consider the circumstances of each conviction, as well as what is specifically in need of proving in the current charge, rather than the general nature of offending, such as violence offences or sexual offences (*R v Bullen* [2008]). Where the defendant admitted the *actus rea* of murder and so the only question was whether he had the *mens rea* of specific intent, the court in *Bullen* found that since none of his ten previous convictions for violence were offences of specific intent, they would not be of help to show that he had the intent on the evening in question. They may have been admissible to show his propensity to use glasses in fights but that was not specifically relied upon by the prosecution.

▌ R v BEVERLEY [2006]

Basic facts

Defendant had previous convictions for possession of cannabis with intent to supply (from 2000) and possession of cannabis (from 2003). Were these admissible under s 101(1)(d) for the offence of conspiracy to import cocaine from Jamaica?

Relevance

The court held that they were not. Here while the first conviction involved intent to supply it concerned a form of dealing wholly different in scale and nature from this conspiracy. Assuming that the convictions established a propensity to commit drugs offences it was doubtful whether on the facts that propensity made it more likely that the defendant committed the conspiracy offence.

While offences falling within the same category or description may more easily demonstrate a propensity for a particular offence, the *Hanson* test will still need to be applied on the facts. Similarly, where a conviction does not fall within the category this is no prohibition to its being adduced. (See *R v Weir* [2005] where charged with sexual assault by touching a girl under the age of 13 (s 7 SOA 2003) the defendant argued that since his previous caution for taking an indecent photograph of a child did not fall within the Secretary of State's category it was inadmissible. Not so held the court as categorisation is only the start.)

It is also important that when a request is made to adduce evidence of previous convictions and that there are weaknesses in the prosecution case, that the judge defers ruling on that point until the conclusion of the prosecution case (*R v Gyima* [2007]).

Propensity to be untruthful

Propensity to be untruthful relates to the way in which the defendant has or is currently conducting his defence. Bad character evidence will be potentially admissible to demonstrate the defendant's propensity to be untruthful so that he cannot be regarded as a credible witness. Under s 103(1)(b), propensity becomes admissible to prove untruthfulness, provided that the prosecution contends that the defendant's case is untruthful in some respect (*R v Somanathan*) and such evidence would not therefore be admissible to prove a propensity to be untruthful where it is not alleged that the defendant's case is untruthful in any respect (s 103(1)(b)).

First of all it is necessary to ask what evidence allows the gateway to open (ie to be applicable) and then what bad character evidence is admissible once open. A simple denial of guilt should not be sufficient to allow admittance of bad character evidence, but if the defendant lies to the police or it is part of the prosecution case that he has, then the gateway will be opened. Once applicable the court in *Hanson* suggested that admissible evidence of bad character would then include convictions for offences of untruthfulness, such as perjury or obtaining property by deception, as well as convictions for any offence where the defendant has entered a not guilty plea and has been convicted (ie he was not believed by the jury). In *R v Campbell* [2007], however, the Court of Appeal held:

> the only circumstance in which there is likely to be an important issue as to whether a Defendant has a propensity to tell lies is where telling lies is an element of the offence charged. Even then, the propensity to tell lies is only likely to be significant if the lying is in the context of committing criminal offences, in which case the evidence is likely to be admissible under s 103(1)(a).

Consequently, the law in this area is in a state of uncertainty at the minute. The Campbell approach would appear to subsume sub-s (b) within sub-s (a).

Excluded evidence

Section 101(3) provides that the court must not admit evidence that is relevant to an important matter in issue between the defendant and his prosecution if, on application by the defendant to exclude it, it appears to the court that the admission of the evidence would have such an adverse effect on the fairness of the proceedings that the court ought not to admit it. Once relevance has been established, the judge should then perform a balancing exercise in order to determine whether the evidence would have such an adverse effect on the fairness of the proceedings that the court ought not to admit it (*R v Somanathan* [2005]). In *R v Tirnaveanu* [2007] the Court of Appeal held that the trial judge had been right to admit the disputed evidence as it was relevant to whether it was the defendant who had committed the offence which meant it was admissible under s 101(1)(d).

The issue of cross-admissibility

If a number of offences are founded on the same facts or form part of a series of a similar character then they may be tried as multiple counts on the same indictment. Section 112(2) stipulates that the bad character provisions have effect as if each offence were charged in separate proceedings. Thus if two or more similar incidents occur with different complainants (eg a dentist committing a similar sexual assault on his patients (*R v Chopra* [2006])), each complainant's evidence must be treated as bad character to be used as evidence that the defendant committed the other offences, and so must be admissible by one of the gateways. This is the issue of cross-admissibility and there are four possibilities:

(a) the evidence under s 101(1)(d) is cross-admissible meaning that the jury can use the evidence of propensity for all of the counts;

(b) the propensity evidence is not cross-admissible;

(c) a combination of some is cross-admissible and some is not; or

(d) the judge will order that the offences are to be tried separately before different juries and thus avoiding undue prejudice.

▶ R v CHOPRA [2006]

Basic facts

A dentist was accused of indecently assaulting three teenage patients in the course of an examination.

Relevance

Due to the similarities between the three complainants' accounts the court held that they were each cross-admissible bad character evidence for each other. The court held: 'Where propensity was advanced by way of multiple complaints, none of which had yet been proved, and whether they were proved or not was the question which the jury had to answer, that was a different case from that in which propensity was advanced through proof of a previous conviction. However, the 2003 Act governed all evidence of bad character, not only conclusive or undisputable evidence. In a case of the kind in the instant case, the critical question for the judge was whether or not the evidence of one complainant was relevant as going, or being capable of going, to establish propensity to commit offences of the kind charged. Not all evidence of other misbehaviour would by any means do so. There had to be sufficient connection between the facts of the several allegations for it properly to be capable of saying that they might establish propensity to offend in the manner charged.

In cases of multiple similar complaints the proposition which the jury had to consider was not that it was not possible to have independent similar false complaints, but rather that each similar complaint made each other similar complaint the more likely.'

In *R v Freeman*, *R v Crawford* [2008] the perpetrator of the offences charged displayed a very similar modus operandi in street muggings of lone females of which the defendant had previously been convicted three times, in the same geographic location. Consequently the court held that the previous convictions could be admitted, but also the bad character shown in the two offences being tried was cross-admissible.

5 It has substantial probative value in relation to an important matter in issue between the defendant and a co-defendant (s 101(1)(e))

Only a co-defendant and not the prosecution can adduce evidence of a defendant's bad character under this section. Once a defendant has given evidence against a co-accused, any subsequent cross-examination of the defendant will be restricted to that which is 'relevant to a matter in issue' and is subject to the 'enhanced relevance test'. Where the notice requirements to adduce bad character evidence have not been complied with the court may exclude such evidence of the defence under Rule 35(8) of the Criminal Procedure Rules 1995 (see *R v Musone* [2007] where the defendant sought to ambush the co-defendant by adducing evidence of a confession apparently given by the co-defendant to a separate murder 12 years previous for which he was acquitted).

Propensity to be untruthful

Where evidence relates to a co-defendant's propensity to be untruthful, s 104(1) provides that evidence which is relevant to the question whether the defendant has a propensity to be untruthful is admissible only if the nature or conduct of his defence is such as to undermine the co-defendant's defence and where the question of that co-defendant's truthfulness is truly relevant to the case for the defendant. The statute does not limit the bad character evidence to only that of past lying in the witness box, and so evidence may be admissible of a defendant's proven history of untruthful dealing with other people if it has substantial probative value on an issue arising between the relevant parties (*R v Jarvis* [2008]), or even wider still in *R v Lawson* [2007]) the court held that the witness' unreliability may be 'capable of being shown by conduct which does not involve an offence of untruthfulness; it may be capable of being shown by widely differing conduct, ranging from large scale drug – or people – trafficking via housebreaking to criminal violence'. While the section shares the same language as s 101(1)(d), the meaning appears to be defined differently by the courts.

6 It is evidence to correct a false impression given by the defendant (s 101(1)(f))

Section 105(1)(a) provides that a defendant gives a false impression if he is responsible for making an express or implied assertion which is apt to give the court a false or misleading impression about himself. Sub-sections 4 and 5 provide that such a false impression can be made by conduct, including dress or appearance. Section 105(2) further provides that a defendant is treated as being responsible for the making of an assertion if:

(a) the assertion is made by the defendant in the proceedings (whether or not in evidence given by him);

(b) the assertion was made by the defendant–
    (i) on being questioned under caution, before charge, about the offence with which he is charged, or
    (ii) on being charged with the offence or officially informed that he might be prosecuted for it, and the evidence of the assertion is given in the proceedings;

(c) the assertion is made by a witness called by the defendant;

(d) the assertion is made by the defendant that is intended to elicit it, or is likely to do so; or

(e) the assertion was made by a person out of court, and the defendant adduces evidence of it in the proceedings.

Once a defendant has given a false impression of himself, the prosecution may rebut with bad character evidence but 'only if it goes no further than is necessary to correct the false impression' (s 105(6)). This is a proportionality criterion between the false impression given and the bad character evidence allowed in rebuttal. In addition, s 78 PACE can be relied upon to exclude prosecution evidence which would be admissible under s 105 (*R v Weir and Others* [2005]).

Disassociation

Section 105(3) provides that a defendant who would otherwise be treated as responsible for the making of an assertion shall not be so treated if he withdraws it or disassociates himself from it. But a confession extracted in cross-examination where a defendant was not telling the truth in his examination-in-chief would not normally amount to a withdrawal or disassociation (*R v Renda* [2005]). If telling the truth itself is not enough to correct the false impression, the provision appears to have a rather more punitive effect than might at first appear.

▶ R v RENDA [2005]

Basic facts

During his examination-in-chief the defendant gave evidence untruthfully that he had been injured as a soldier in the Queen's armed forces and was currently in regular employment as a security guard. In cross-examination he was forced to reveal the truth. The question was whether in being forced to reveal the truth he had sufficiently disassociated himself from the misleading assertion.

Relevance

The court held that he had not; rather than it having been a positive decision to correct the false impression the defendant was obliged to concede that he had been misleading the jury. Consequently even though the truth was eventually told, bad character evidence was admissible.

7 The defendant has made an attack on another person's character (s 101(1)(g))

Section 106(1) provides that a defendant makes an attack on another person's character if:

(a) he adduces evidence attacking the other person's character;

(b) he (or any legal representative appointed under s 38(4) of the Youth Justice and Criminal Evidence Act 1999 (c 23)) asks questions in cross-examination that are intended to elicit such evidence, or are likely to do so; or

(c) evidence is given of an imputation about the other person made by the defendant on being questioned under caution, before charge, about the offence with which he is charged, or on being charged with the offence or officially informed that he might be prosecuted for it.

Section 106(2) provides that evidence which attacks another person's character means evidence to the effect that the other person has committed an offence, whether a different offence from the one with which the defendant is charged or the same one, or has behaved, or is disposed to behave, in a reprehensible way. It is irrelevant to s 106 if the attack is necessary for the defendant's defence, although it might be an issue of relevance for the discretion to exclude in s 101(3). Attacks on the police investigation of the offence, to suggest fabrication of the charge or evidence for example, falls within s 98 in that it is not evidence of bad character; but it is understood that a defendant will nevertheless be caught by s 101(1)(g) for 'attacking another person's character' and subsequently his bad character may be adduced (*R v Williams* [2007]). Unlike s 101(1)(f) there is no proportionality criterion for the bad character evidence adduced under s 101(1)(g).

Accusations that the complainant is 'not a witness of truth and has some ulterior motive in making and indeed pursuing this complaint' (*R v Samanathan* [2005]), 'would have slept with anyone' (*R v Ball* [2005]) and 'was attacking me everywhere' (*R v Lamaletie* [2008] on a claim of self-defence to assault).

The court in *R v Nelson* [2006] issued a warning to prosecutors regarding the use of spurious attacks made by the defendant in interview, for example, of non-witnesses purely to open the gateway.

Excluded evidence

Section 101(3) provides that the court must not admit evidence where the defendant has made an attack on another person's character if, on application by the defendant to exclude it, it appears to the court that the admission of the evidence would have such an adverse effect on the fairness of the proceedings that the court ought not to admit it. There is no requirement in the Act that the attack on the other person's character should be untrue or unfounded. Where it can be shown that those allegations are true, however, then the court may exercise its discretion and exclude the evidence of bad character on the basis that it is fair to do so.

A right of appeal exists for the prosecution against evidential rulings that significantly weaken the prosecution case under ss 62 and 63 CJA 2003.

Once evidence has been admitted through a particular gateway, to what purpose can evidence then be used?

Once evidence of bad character has been admitted through one of the 'gateways' in the Criminal Justice Act 2003 (s 101(1)), the use to which it could be put depends upon the matters to which it was relevant rather than upon the gateway through which it was admitted (*R v Highton*; *R v Nguyen*; and *R v Carp* [2005]). Essentially the gateways determine admissibility but not the use to which the evidence can be put once admitted. In *R v Lafayette* [2008] the Court of Appeal appears to have curtailed the *Highton* approach as regards s 101(1)(g) for evidence admitted through that section but which would not have been admissible through s 101(1)(d). The Court suggested that such evidence would not ordinarily be open to use as propensity evidence.

Discretion to exclude under s 78 of PACE

Section 101(3) is applicable to only evidence adduced under sub-ss 101(1)(d) and (g) and is designed to reflect the existing position under s 78 of PACE, under which the judge or magistrates assess the probative value of the evidence to an issue in the case and the prejudicial effect of admitting it, and excludes the evidence where it would be unfair to admit it. However, the test to be applied under s 101(3) is stricter than that under s 78 of PACE in that under s 78 the court *may* refuse to admit the evidence, whereas under s 101(3) the court *must not* admit such evidence if it would have such an adverse effect on the fairness of the proceedings. Other than in s 101(1)(e), which is subject to the 'enhanced relevance' test in any event, it is submitted that s 78 of PACE will continue to apply to the other gateways.

Stopping the case where evidence is contaminated

Section 107(5)(b) provides that evidence is contaminated where it is false or misleading in any respect, or is different from what it would otherwise have been (*R v Card* [2006]). Section 107(1) provides that if during a defendant's trial before a judge and jury for an offence, evidence of his bad character has been admitted under any of the paragraphs (c) to (g) of s 101(1), and the court is satisfied at any time after the close of the case for the prosecution that the evidence is contaminated and the contamination is such that, considering the importance of the evidence to the case against the defendant, his conviction of the offence would be unsafe, the court must direct the jury to acquit the defendant of the offence, or if it considers that there ought to be a retrial, discharge the jury. There is no explicit duty to stop proceedings, however, where the evidence 'might' be contaminated, which suggests that the evidence be left to the jury to determine its weight.

Effect of s 107

This provision does not affect any existing court powers in relation to ordering an acquittal or discharging a jury. Instead the effect of s 107 is to further supplement those powers by conferring a duty on the judge to stop the case if the contamination is such that, considering the importance of the evidence to the case, a conviction would be unsafe.

Offences committed by a defendant when a child

Section 108(2) provides that in proceedings for an offence committed or alleged to have been committed by the defendant when aged 21 or over, evidence of his conviction for an offence when under the age of 14 is not admissible unless:

(a) both of the offences are triable only on indictment, and

(b) the court is satisfied that the interests of justice require the evidence to be admissible.

These factors are *additional* to those factors outlined in s 101 (defendant's bad character) as discussed above.

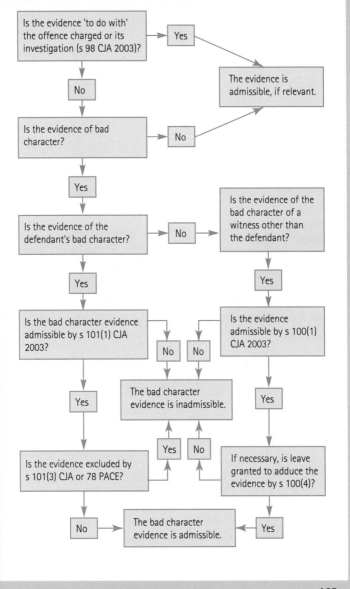

OTHER CONSIDERATIONS

NOTICE

The prosecution must give notice to the defence if it seeks to rely on bad character evidence. This is irrespective of how it is presented to the court and the notice requirement will equally apply if the prosecution seek to adduce such information by way of cross-examination (s 111(2)). If notice is not given, then the court may exercise its powers with respect to costs (s 111(4)).

RELEVANT RULING

Relevant ruling means a ruling on whether an item of evidence is evidence of a person's bad character and whether such evidence is admissible under s 100 (non-defendant's bad character) or s 101 (defendant's bad character). The court may also make a ruling under s 101(3) and decide that it would be unfair to admit evidence or under s 107 where the court decides to stop the case where evidence is contaminated.

COURT'S DUTY TO GIVE REASONS FOR RULINGS

Section 110 provides that where a court makes a relevant ruling, it must state in open court (but in the absence of the jury, if there is one), its reasons for the ruling. If it is a Magistrates' Court, it must cause the ruling and the reasons for it to be entered in the register of the court's proceedings.

PROOF OF CONVICTIONS AND DETAIL ALLOWED

Proof of a criminal conviction is by way of the certificate of the conviction under ss 73 and 74 PACE 1984. Where a party wishes to rely on the details of the previous convictions this intention will need to have been included within the notice to adduce evidence of bad character. The parties should try to agree to a set of facts to present to the court, but where this is not possible the facts will need to be proved possibly by a witness statement of the complainant to the previous incident (*R v Humphris* [2005]). If the witness is unavailable to give a first-hand account the statement could be proved by a hearsay exception (including s 114(1)(d) CJA 2003).

SPENT CONVICTIONS

Criminal offences are excluded from the scope of the Rehabilitation of Offenders Act 1974, but a 2002 Practice Direction (replacing the earlier 1974 practice direction) requires courts to have regard to the spirit of the 1974 Act. Generally, therefore, courts should not allow reference to spent convictions (para. 6.5 'when such reference can reasonably be avoided') except on the authority of the judge and only in the interests of justice. Unless such spent convictions are relevant to the current charge under s 101, convictions old enough to be spent will not carry much weight, and may be excluded under s 101(3).

ASSUMPTION OF TRUTH

Section 109 provides that any reference to relevance or probative value of evidence is on the assumption that such evidence is true. In assessing the relevance or probative value of an item of evidence, a court may not assume that the evidence is true if it appears, on the basis of any material before the court (including any evidence it decides to hear on the matter), that no court or jury could reasonably find it to be true.

CRIMINAL STATUTES ALLOWING BAD CHARACTER EVIDENCE

A number of statutes specifically allow the admissibility of bad character evidence to prove part of an offence, in these situations that evidence would be admissible regardless of the CJA regime but its uses would be limited by the provisions of the particular statute concerned.

Section 103 Road Traffic Act 1988 allows proof that the defendant was disqualified from driving at the relevant time for the offence of driving whilst disqualified. The defendant's character is not otherwise relevant. Similarly, under s 1 Street Offences Act 1959 previous police cautions or convictions for prostitution are admissible to prove that the defendant was a 'common prostitute' (ie one who has previously been cautioned/convicted of prostitution) where it is an offence to 'loiter or solicit in a street or public place for the purpose of prostitution'.

Section 21(1) Firearms Act 1968 provides that 'it is an offence for a person who has been sentenced to custody for life or to imprisonment for a term of three years or more, or the equivalent for a young offender, to have a firearm or ammunition in his possession at any time'. Thus a previous conviction having a sentence that fulfils the condition will be admissible.

Section 27(3) Theft Act 1968 allows bad character evidence of a previous conviction within the last five years for theft or handling stolen goods on a charge of handling. The value of the bad character evidence is in aiding in the proof of the defendant's knowledge or belief that the goods on the current charge were stolen.

You should now be confident that you would be able to tick all of the boxes on the checklist at the beginning of this chapter. To check your knowledge of Character evidence why not visit the companion website and take the Multiple Choice Question test. Check your understanding of the terms and vocabulary used in this chapter with the flashcard glossary.

Opinion evidence

The main topics of importance are:

(a) the circumstances in which opinion evidence is generally admissible;

(b) analysing the basis on which an opinion has been given; and

(c) the extent to which the evidence of psychiatrists or psychologists is admissible in criminal trials.

WHEN IS OPINION EVIDENCE ADMISSIBLE?

The fundamental rule is that witnesses testify about facts of which they have perceived and not about the opinions they have formed from facts. The reason for this is the idea that it is the job of the 'tribunal of fact' (a judge or, very occasionally, a jury in a civil case, and magistrates or a jury in a criminal case) to hear the evidence, find facts, and make inferences from them. For this reason a witness should not generally be asked to give his opinion about what another witness has said (*R v Windass* [1989]).

By s 3(2) of the Civil Evidence Act 1972, a person called as a witness in civil proceedings may give a statement of opinion on any matter on which he is not qualified to give expert evidence, if that statement is made as a way of conveying relevant facts personally perceived by him. In criminal proceedings admissibility is governed by s 118 Criminal Justice Act 2003 and Part 33 Criminal Procedure Rules.

The main exception to the fundamental rule is that in both civil and criminal cases an expert may give evidence of his opinion where the matters on which he testifies are likely to be outside the experience of judge or jury. The rationale for admitting expert evidence was stated in *R v Luttrell* [2004], such that:

> 'For expert evidence to be admissible, two conditions must be satisfied: first, that study or experience will give a witness's opinion an authority which the opinion of one not so qualified will lack; and secondly the witness must be so qualified to express the opinion.'

In *R v Stockwell* [1993], the Court of Appeal said that in each case it is for the judge to decide:

- whether the issue is one on which the court could be assisted by expert evidence;

- whether the expert tendered has the expertise to provide such evidence.

While a witness giving such evidence should be skilled in the subject, there are no restrictions on the manner in which that skill has to be acquired. The evidence of a person without professional qualifications can be admitted, provided that the judge is satisfied that the witness is sufficiently skilled (*R v Silverlock* [1894]). So, a witness who has acquired his expertise in the course of his daily work may give expert evidence even though he lacks paper qualifications. See, for example, *R v Murphy* [1980], where a police constable who was a traffic accident expert was allowed to give evidence of his opinion as to the nature of a collision, the course of one of the vehicles involved and other matters said to be deducible from marks in the road and damage to the vehicles. Also see *R (on the application of Crown Prosecution Service) v Sedgemoor Justices* [2007], although a blood sample analyst was not an 'authorised analyst' within the meaning of s 16(7) of the Road Traffic Offenders Act 1988, the evidence by way of witness statement was admissible.

A witness who is otherwise not specially qualified may be an 'expert *ad hoc*' where he has special knowledge acquired by study of materials that are relevant in a particular case, such as video recordings or photographs (*R v Clare and Peach* [1995]).

Although it is clear that the object of expert evidence is to provide the court with information that is outside the experience of judge or jury, there is little authority on how to determine whether particular information falls within this class. A case where a problem did arise (though it was not the central problem) was *R v Stagg* [1994], where the trial judge doubted whether evidence obtained from the technique known as 'psychological profiling' was expert evidence of a kind recognised by the courts.

THE BASIS OF THE OPINION

An expert gives his opinion on the basis of facts in a particular case but those facts must themselves be proved by admissible evidence. However, if the rule against hearsay was strictly applied, an expert would often be prevented from giving an opinion because his reasoning and conclusions would be governed by matters that he had learned in the course of his training and experience, either from what he had read, or from others who share his specialisation. The courts have therefore relaxed the hearsay rule to take this into account

(*Abbey National Mortgages plc v Key Surveyors Nationwide Ltd* [1996] and s 118 Criminal Justice Act 2003).

Experts may support their opinions by referring to articles, letters, journals and other materials, whether published or not, when giving their testimony. Where they have done so, however, this should be mentioned in their evidence so that it can be taken into account when considering the probative worth of their opinion as a whole (*R v Abadom* [1983]). This is particularly key when the expert evidence relates to a new scientific technique (see *R v Kempster* [2008] on earprint analysis).

Sometimes the primary facts of a case are not established by the expert himself, but by other members of a team, which the expert leads. In such a case, the evidence of the other relevant team members must be available (in the absence of formal admissions), so that the primary facts can all be proved by admissible evidence (*R v Jackson* [1996]).

By s 30(1) of the Criminal Justice Act 1988, an 'expert report' (that is, a written report by a person dealing wholly or mainly with matters on which he is, or, if living, would be, qualified to give expert evidence) shall be admissible as evidence in criminal proceedings, whether or not the person making it attends to give oral evidence. If it is proposed that the person making the report shall not give oral evidence, the report shall be admissible only with leave of the court (but it seems most unlikely that a court would allow an expert report to be adduced without calling the maker if the opposing party had a genuine desire to cross-examine on it).

EVIDENCE FROM PSYCHIATRISTS AND PSYCHOLOGISTS

To some extent judges recognise that a psychiatrist or psychologist may be able to provide useful testimony about matters that are outside the experience of judge or jurors (see, eg, *DPP v A and BC Chewing Gum Ltd* [1968], which concerned the effect of certain articles on children, and *R v Morris* [1998], in which the Court of Appeal held that expert evidence is required where it is alleged that psychiatric illness or injury resulted from a defendant's non-physical assault).

There is also a fear that psychiatric experts will usurp the role of the jury or other triers of fact unless a clear line is drawn between abnormal and normal mental states. One effect of this has been to draw a distinction between expert evidence relevant to the reliability of a confession and expert evidence relevant to *mens rea*. Judges regularly admit psychiatric or psychological evidence when considering submissions about the admissibility of confessions, because the mental condition of the defendant at the time of interview is one of the circumstances to be considered under s 76(2)(b) of the Police and Criminal Evidence Act 1984 (*R v Raghip* [1991]). In *R v Walker* [1998], it was held that nothing limits the form of mental or psychological condition on which a defendant can rely to show that his confession is unreliable. However, in *R v O'Brian and Others* [2000], the Court of Appeal said that, while it had been accepted that expert evidence was admissible if it demonstrated some abnormality relevant to the reliability of a defendant's confession:

- the abnormal disorder must not only be of the type which might render a confession unreliable, but there must also be a very significant deviation from the norm; and

- there should be a history pre-dating the making of admissions which was not based solely on an account given by the defendant and which pointed to or explained the abnormality.

In *R v Coles* [1995], the Court of Appeal held that expert evidence is inadmissible to enable a jury to reach a decision about the existence of *mens rea, unless related to the mental health or psychiatric state of the defendant*. Thus, jurors have been held to be sufficiently acquainted with how ordinary people are likely to react to the stresses and strains of life (*R v Turner* [1975]; but see also *R v Lowery* [1974]). Similarly, they are not allowed to have expert evidence to tell them whether a person, not suffering from some defect or abnormality of mind, is likely to be telling the truth (*R v Mackenney* [1981]).

There has also recently been issue about whether expert witnesses are immune from disciplinary proceedings in relation to the evidence that they have given. In *Meadow v General Medical Council* [2006], the Court of Appeal ruled that there was no reason to extend full immunity to all fitness to practise proceedings. However in this case the expert was found not guilty as he was guilty of professional misconduct but not serious professional misconduct. The Court of Appeal said that the expert had not intended to mislead the Court; he believed (mistakenly) that the statistical evidence was valid.

Where psychiatric evidence does not suggest any organic or psychiatric connection between the defendant's medical condition and his inability at the material time to commit the crime, the evidence will be inadmissible, since it will go to prove the probability of the defendant's truthfulness, as opposed to providing relevant information likely to be outside the experience of a court or jury (*R v Loughran* [1999]).

EXPERT EVIDENCE ON THE 'ULTIMATE ISSUE'

Whether an expert could give his opinion on the ultimate issue, that is, the very question to be decided by the court, was a vexed question for a long time. So far as civil proceedings are concerned, the question is now answered by s 3 of the Civil Evidence Act 1972, which provides that, where a person is called as a witness in civil proceedings, his opinion on any relevant matter, including an issue in the proceedings, shall be admissible if he is qualified to give expert evidence on it.

In criminal cases, evidence of an expert on a particular matter is sometimes excluded on the ground that it would be providing an opinion on the ultimate issue (see, eg, *R v Theodosi* [1993]), but the rule is frequently ignored. Thus, in *R v Stockwell* [1993], the Court of Appeal said that an expert is called to give his opinion and should be allowed to do so. What is important is that the judge should make it clear to the jury that they are not bound by an expert's opinion.

CIVIL PROCEEDINGS

Unlike in criminal proceedings (where expert evidence is only admissible if it falls *outside* of the court's experience), Part 35 of the Civil Procedure Rules 1988 (CPR) provides that even where a matter does not fall outside the court's experience, the court is empowered to exclude, restrict or limit the nature of the expert evidence.

COURT'S PERMISSION

Part 35 of the CPR requires the court to restrict expert evidence to that which is reasonably required to resolve the proceedings and accordingly the court's permission is required either to call an expert or to put an expert's report in evidence. Once such permission is given, evidence will normally be given by written report and the parties will not be entitled to call their expert witnesses to give evidence *unless* the court directs that the experts attend the hearing. Where the parties wish to adduce expert evidence in relation to an issue, the court may select a single joint expert from a list that the parties have prepared or approved, or may direct another method of selecting a single joint expert.

INDIVIDUAL EXPERTS

Part 35 of the CPR further provides that where a single joint expert is not used, the court will direct the parties to exchange expert reports at the same time on a specified date. If a party fails to disclose an expert's report in accordance with the court's direction, the party will not be able to rely on the report or to call the expert at the trial without the court's permission. A party is entitled to put written questions about the report to the expert within 28 days of its service. The purpose of these questions would be to clarify any issues and the expert's answers would be treated as part of the report. If the expert fails to provide answers to the questions asked, then the court may direct that the party who instructed the expert cannot rely on his evidence.

Note: once disclosed, any party at the trial may use an expert's report.

ADDITIONAL POWERS UNDER PART 35 OF THE CPR

The court may direct one party to provide another party with information (for example, blood test results), which is not otherwise accessible to that other party. Similarly, the court may direct discussions between the experts (in situations where parties have their own experts) in an attempt to identify and agree the expert issues.

CONTENTS OF THE REPORT

Duty of the expert

Part 35 of the CPR provides that the expert is under a duty to help the court. This duty overrides the expert's duty to the party who instructed him and the understanding and compliance of this duty needs to be reiterated in his report.

Qualifications/instructions/literature/research
The report must specify the expert's qualifications and provide a summary of the expert's instructions. It is also a requirement that the report specifies the literature, research, etc, that the expert has relied on when making the report.

Conclusions
The report must provide the expert's conclusions. If there is a 'range' of views, the report must summarise these and must indicate why the expert arrived at a particular opinion or conclusion.

Statement of truth
A 'statement of truth' must verify the report.

Inaccurate or incomplete report
If there are reasonable grounds to consider that the summary of instructions contained in the expert's report is inaccurate or incomplete, the court may order disclosure of documents or questioning of witnesses in relation to the instructions.

Failure to comply with the requirements of Part 35 of the CPR
If an expert's report does not comply with the requirements of Part 35 of the CPR and/or the expert witness does not appear to have complied with his duty to the court, the court may exclude the expert's evidence.

You should now be confident that you would be able to tick all of the boxes on the checklist at the beginning of this chapter. To check your knowledge of Opinion evidence why not visit the companion website and take the Multiple Choice Question test. Check your understanding of the terms and vocabulary used in this chapter with the flashcard glossary.

11

Privilege and public interest immunity

This chapter deals with reasons for excluding evidence that are unlike any previously encountered. Other exclusionary rules or principles have as the reason for their existence the need to secure a fair trial. The justification for the rules relating to privilege and public interest immunity has nothing to do with the fairness of the trial but with some other benefit that is thought to be more important. The rules about privilege and public interest immunity acknowledge that the public have interests that must occasionally be allowed to prevail over their interest in securing fair trials, at which all relevant and otherwise admissible evidence can be heard. Although these topics have this understanding in common, they operate differently. A *privilege* is a *right which the law gives to a person* allowing him to refuse to testify about a particular matter or to withhold a document. Effect is given to *public interest immunity* by means of a *power which the courts have* to exclude evidence on the ground that disclosure of information would be damaging to the general good.

There are three main privileges:

- privilege against self-incrimination;

- legal professional privilege;

- privilege arising from statements made 'without prejudice'.

PRIVILEGE AGAINST SELF-INCRIMINATION

Section 14(1) of the Civil Evidence Act 1968, which is declaratory of the common law (*Rio Tinto Zinc Corp v Westinghouse Electric Corp* [1978]), describes this privilege as the right of a person in any legal proceedings, other than criminal proceedings, to refuse to answer any question or produce any document or thing if to do so would tend to expose that person to proceedings for an offence or for the recovery of a penalty. Section 14 extends the privilege in civil proceedings to protect a person's spouse or civil partner. At common law, the privilege was restricted to the person claiming it.

The privilege has to be claimed, on oath, by the person who wishes to rely on it. Thus, it cannot be claimed on discovery in a civil action by a solicitor on his client's behalf (*Downie v Coe* [1997]).

Proceedings for civil contempt are proceedings for the 'recovery of a penalty' for the purpose of s 14 of the Civil Evidence Act 1968 (*Cobra Golf v Rata*

[1997]). The privilege is available even in respect of the risk of contempt proceedings in the action in which the privilege is claimed (*Memory Corp plc v Sidhu* [2000]).

Statutes have abolished the privilege in certain cases. Sometimes, that has been done by providing that a person may be questioned, but that only a limited use may be made of his answers (see, eg, s 31 of the Theft Act 1968; s 9 of the Criminal Damage Act 1971; s 98 of the Children Act 1989). At one time, it was thought that the scope of the privilege could be cut down by the courts in a similar way, but it is now accepted that where statute has not limited the use to which such evidence can be put, the civil courts have no power to impose a limit of their own devising (*Bishopsgate Investment Management Ltd v Maxwell* [1993]).

As well as cases where the privilege has been expressly removed by statute, there are cases where statutes have impliedly removed it. See, for example, *Re London United Investments plc* [1992] in relation to examinations under s 432 of the Companies Act 1985; *Bank of England v Riley* [1992] in relation to examinations under the Banking Act 1987; *Bishopsgate Investment Management Ltd v Maxwell* [1993] in relation to inquiries under s 235 or 236 of the Insolvency Act 1986 and *O'Halloran and Francis v UK* [2008] in relation to s 172(2) Road Traffic Act 1988.

ARTICLE 6 OF THE EUROPEAN CONVENTION ON HUMAN RIGHTS

In certain situations, statute expressly or impliedly removes the privilege against self-incrimination without affording any alternative means of protection. The effect of this is that a person is compelled to provide evidence, which is later used in criminal proceedings against him. This provision is likely to result in a violation of Art 6 of the European Convention on Human Rights (*Saunders v UK* [1996]). In order to avoid future violations of Art 6, a number of these statutory provisions have been amended by the Youth Justice and Criminal Evidence Act 1999. An example of such an amendment can be seen in the examination of persons by the Department of Trade and Industry. Here the prosecution cannot adduce evidence concerning the defendant's answers to inspectors' questions, nor can he be questioned about those answers in subsequent criminal proceedings.

DEFENDANT'S SILENCE UPON ACCUSATION

The silence of the defendant may amount to a confession if it can be construed as an adoption of an accusation by the person against whom it is made. The circumstances must be that the accuser and defendant are on equal terms, the defendant remained silent when an accusation was made, and the circumstances were such that remaining silent could be inferred as an acceptance of the accusation. And so answers to a police officer will not usually fulfil the requirements (*Parkes v R* [1976]). In *Parkes* the defendant was found over the dead body of the witness' daughter with a knife in his hand (she had been stabbed). The mother said 'What did she do to you – why did you stab her?' and the defendant did not reply. She hit him twice and seized him, saying that she would keep him there until the police arrived, at which point he tried to stab her with the knife. In these circumstances the defendant's reactions to the accusations, including his silence, were evidence that the jury could consider in deciding whether the defendant had murdered the girl.

DEFENDANT'S FAILURE TO ANSWER QUESTIONS OR MENTION FACTS

Under the Criminal Justice and Public Order Act 1994, there may be circumstances in which a suspect's silence, though not amounting to a confession, may be used as the basis for making inferences at trial.

SECTION 34 OF THE CJPOA

A court or jury may draw such inferences as appear proper from evidence that the defendant failed, on being questioned under caution, or on being charged with the offence, to mention any fact relied on in his defence if it was a fact which, in the circumstances existing at the time, he could reasonably have been expected to mention. The section applies to questioning by police officers, but also to questioning by other persons charged with the duty of investigating offences or charging offenders (s 34(4)).

When deciding whether a defendant could reasonably have been expected to mention a particular fact, consideration has to be taken of the *actual* defendant, with such qualities, knowledge, apprehensions and advice as he had at the time and in the circumstances existing at the time; notably the time of day, whether the defendant was sober or tired (*R v Argent* [1997]).

❭ R v ARGENT [1997]

Basic facts

Argent appealed against conviction and sentence of ten years' imprisonment for manslaughter. Following his arrest he declined to answer questions in police interviews on legal advice. The trial judge declined to admit police evidence of the first interview but admitted the second interview on the grounds that it had been preceded by a positive identification. The defence argued that the judge was wrong when directing the jury that it was open to them to draw an inference from Argent's silence.

Relevance

Sets out six conditions that have to be fulfilled before a jury can draw inferences in terms of the Criminal Justice and Public Order Act 1994 s 34(2)(d), from an accused's failure to mention during police questioning any fact which he subsequently relied on in his defence. They offer clear guidance on this issue and you should be aware of them.

If a defendant says that he refused to answer questions on legal advice, that, by itself, is unlikely to be a sufficient reason for his failure to mention facts subsequently relied on in his defence. In practice, a defendant will have to go further and provide, either through his own testimony or that of his legal adviser, the reasons for the advice (*R v Condron* [1997]).

❭ R v CONDRON [1997]

Basic facts

The defendants were arrested for supplying drugs. At the police station their solicitor considered them unfit to be interviewed because of drug withdrawal symptoms. They were advised not to answer questions. However, the police doctor considered that they were fit for interview. The defendants made no comment but at their trial admitted their addiction to heroin but denied supplying the drug. The judge rejected the submission that since the defendants' solicitor had advised them not to answer questions no adverse inferences could be drawn (s 34 of the Criminal Justice and Public Order Act 1994) and that evidence of the police interview should be excluded. When the judge summed up to the jury he told them that it was a matter for them to decide whether any adverse inference should be drawn against the defendants. The defendants were convicted.

Relevance

The jury should be given an opportunity to consider whether the defendant's refusal to answer questions has reasonable grounds. The burden of proving guilt beyond reasonable doubt still remained on the prosecution and that the defendant was entitled not to mention a fact later relied on and an inference from the failure to mention it could not on its own prove guilt.

In *R v Gayle* [1999], the Court of Appeal held that s 34 does not apply to silence at an interview that took place in breach of any of the provisions of the Codes. By s 34(2A) of the CJPOA, where the accused was at an authorised place of detention, sub-ss (1) and (2) do not apply if he had not been allowed an opportunity to consult a solicitor prior to being questioned, charged or informed that he might be prosecuted.

The section requires that the defendant must have failed to mention some fact *that he relies on in his defence*. In *R v Moshaid* [1998], the defendant gave a 'no comment' interview and, at trial, gave no evidence and called no witnesses. The Court of Appeal held that s 34 did not apply because the defendant had not failed to mention 'any fact relied on in his defence at trial', but this was an unusual case. The House of Lords has recently said that 'fact' should be given a broad meaning (*R v Webber* [2004]). Thus, a belief formed by the accused upon the basis of information given to him by another may amount to a 'fact' (*R v Lydiate* [2004]). The accused may rely upon a fact by giving evidence of that fact himself or by adducing such evidence via examination-in-chief or cross-examination of other witnesses. The accused may also rely upon a fact in his defence if it is put to the court in counsel's closing speech (*R v Webber* [2004]). Facts relied on may be established by prosecution witnesses in cross-examination or even during examination-in-chief, as well as by defence evidence (*R v Bowers and Others* [1998]). Note also where an accused gives a prepared statement to police but makes no comment in interview, this can amount to mentioning a fact (*R v Knight* [2003]).

The question of whether an accused has relied on a particular fact and, if so, whether he failed to mention it at interview is one of fact for the jury. There will, however, be cases where it is appropriate for a judge to decide, as a matter of law, whether there is any evidence on which a jury could conclude that either, or both, of these requirements has been satisfied. Where a judge has ruled that there is no such evidence, he should specifically direct the jury that they should not draw any adverse inference from the defendant's silence at interview (*R v McGarry* [1998]).

Where a defendant gives evidence that he refused to answer questions on legal advice, it may amount to a waiver of legal professional privilege. Whether or not the privilege is waived will depend upon the reasonableness of the accused's silence (*R v Condron* [1997]). It is thus irrelevant whether the advice was correct or incorrect, but rather whether it was reasonable for the accused to remain silent having regard to the nature of the advice and the context in which the advice was given. In this situation a lawyer/client privilege may well be waived and the prosecution may, during cross-examination of the accused or indeed his solicitor, explore the basis of, or the reasons for, the advice and the content of the lawyer/client conversation. Similarly, where an accused gives a 'no comment' interview upon the advice of his solicitor, this will not prevent the jury from drawing a s 34 inference if they believe that the accused's silence was because he had no, or no satisfactory, explanation to give which was consistent with his innocence (*R v Hoare* [2004]). Similarly, where he goes further, for example, by eliciting evidence in cross-examination of a statement made to the police after the interview, setting out the grounds on which that advice was given, he will waive the privilege and can be cross-examined about the nature of the advice and the facts on which it was based (*R v Bowden* [1999]). The hearsay rule will be no bar to the admissibility of such evidence because it will be admitted to establish the effect of what was said on the defendant's state of mind when he decided not to answer police questions (*R v Daniel* [1998]; *R v Davis* [1998]).

In *R v Bresa* [2005] the Court of Appeal said that, among the key features of a direction under s 34 of the CJPOA 1994 (adverse inferences) are the following:

(i) there needs to be the striking of a fair balance between telling the jury of a defendant's rights (to remain silent or not to disclose advice), and telling the jury that the defendant has a choice not to rely on those rights;

(ii) there needs to be an accurate identification of the facts which it is alleged a defendant might reasonably have mentioned;

(iii) there needs to be a warning that there must be a case to answer and the jury cannot convict on inference alone;

(iv) there must be a direction to the effect that the key question is whether the jury can be sure that the accused remains silent not because of any advice but because he had no satisfactory explanation to give (per Waller LJ at para 16).

The scope for making inferences under s 34 was considered in *R v Daniel* [1998], which was followed in *R v Beckles and Montague* [1999]. A jury is entitled to draw an adverse inference if they think the defendant's silence can only sensibly be attributed:

■ to his unwillingness to be subjected to further questioning; or

■ to the fact that he had not thought out all the facts; or

■ to the fact that he did not have an innocent explanation to give.

Note: for the jury to draw an inference other than recent fabrication, they require an appropriate direction from the judge (*R v Petkar* [2003]).

The Counter-Terrorism Act 2008 in s 22(9) affords an extension of post-charge questioning where the defendant is charged with a 'terrorism offence', and so adverse inferences can be drawn if he fails to mention facts when questioned if he later relies on them in court.

For the defendant's silence during the trial and the issue of adverse inferences see chapter 4.

ARTICLE 6 OF THE EUROPEAN CONVENTION ON HUMAN RIGHTS

In *Murray v UK* [1996], the European Court of Human Rights stated that a conviction should not be based solely or even mainly upon the accuser's silence. The court went on to say that the right to silence, though not an absolute right, remains a fundamental aspect of the fair trial procedure under Art 6 of the Convention.

SECTIONS 36 AND 37 OF THE CJPOA

These sections deal with inferences that may be drawn, in certain circumstances, from a defendant's failure to account for objects, substances, marks or his own presence in a particular place.

INFERENCES FROM REFUSAL TO PROVIDE SAMPLES

By s 62(10) of PACE, an adverse inference may be drawn from a suspect's refusal, without good cause, to consent to the taking of 'intimate samples' from his body. By s 65 of PACE (as amended by the CJPOA), an 'intimate sample' is:

- a sample of blood, semen or any other tissue fluid, urine or pubic hair;

- a dental impression;

- a swab taken from a person's body orifice other than the mouth.

'Non-intimate samples' may be taken, subject to procedural conditions, without a suspect's consent, and no provision corresponding to s 62(10) is therefore necessary.

EXCLUSION OF EVIDENCE FROM SILENCE

Section 38(6) preserves judicial discretion to exclude evidence of silence in s 78 PACE and the common law.

LEGAL PROFESSIONAL PRIVILEGE

According to Lord Hoffman in *R (on the application of Morgan Grenfell & Co Ltd) v Special Commissioner of Income Tax* [2002] legal professional privilege is a fundamental human right protected by the right of privacy guaranteed by Article 8 of the European Convention of Human Rights. Although in *McE v Prison Service of Northern Ireland and Another* [2009] it was recognised that it is the use of privileged evidence in court that is prohibited, not listening in on the conversation. This case raised a number of concerns surrounding covert surveillance of lawyer/client consultations and the regulations introduced under the Regulation of Investigatory Powers Act 2000 (RIPA).

The scope of legal professional privilege at common law is reflected in s 10 of the Police and Criminal Evidence Act 1984 (PACE) (*R v Central Criminal Court ex p Francis and Francis* [1988]). There are three categories set out in the Act.

SECTION 10(1)(a) OF PACE

Deals with communications between a professional legal adviser and his client (or any person representing his client) which are made in connection with the giving of legal advice to the client. Here, the communication is a two-way system and can be thought of in the form of a straight line, with the client or his agent at one end and the legal adviser at the other. Thus:

Client/agent ←————————————————→ Legal adviser

The legal advice can be of any kind and does not have to be connected with litigation or the prospect of it. The protection is available even where the lawyer is an 'in-house' lawyer advising his employers (*Alfred Crompton Amusement Machines Ltd v Customs & Excise Commissioners* [1972]).

In *Balabel v Air India* [1988], Taylor LJ said that, although the test for a privileged communication was whether it had been made confidentially for the purpose of obtaining legal advice, this purpose was not to be narrowly construed and should be taken to include practical advice about what should be done in the relevant legal context.

In *Three Rivers District Council v Bank of England (No 6)* [2004] Lord Carswell in the House of Lords defined the notion of 'legal advice' broadly, to mean, 'The work of advising a client on the most suitable approach to adopt, assembling material for presentation of his case and taking statements which set out the relevant material in an orderly fashion and omit the irrelevant is to my mind the classic exercise of one of the lawyer's skills. I can see no valid reason why that should cease to be so because the forum is an inquiry or other tribunal which is not a court of law, provided that the advice is given in a legal context: see Lord Scott's opinion at para 42. The skills of a lawyer in assembling the facts and handling the evidence are of importance in that forum as well as a court of law. The availability of competent legal advice will materially assist an inquiry by reducing irrelevance and encouraging the making of proper admissions.'

SECTION 10(1)(b) OF PACE

Deals with communications between lawyer, client *and third parties* for the purpose of pending or contemplated litigation. Thus litigation must be contemplated at the time the document is made in order for it to be privileged (*Wheeler v Le Marchant* [1881]; *Gotha City v Cotheby's* [1998]). The lines of communication can be seen as forming a triangle so as to involve three parties instead of two. Thus:

Third party

Client/agent   Legal adviser

Here, the communications with the third parties, often other professionals such as surveyors, doctors or accountants, will be protected only if the sole or dominant purpose is for use in litigation, pending or contemplated (*Waugh v BRB* [1980]).

Documents obtained for the purpose of obtaining legal advice with respect to pending or contemplated litigation are privileged, even though the litigation is contemplated only by the party seeking the advice, and the other prospective party is unaware that litigation might arise (*Plummers Ltd v Debenhams plc* [1986]).

SECTION 10(1)(c) OF PACE

This covers items enclosed with or referred to in communications of types (a) or (b), provided that the items came into existence in connection with the giving of legal advice and are in the possession of a person who is entitled to possession of them. The point here is that the privilege exists to protect communications between client, legal adviser and, sometimes, third parties. It does not exist to protect evidence from production (*R v King* [1983]).

Copies of original documents are frequently brought into existence in the course of a legal professional relationship. Whether their disclosure can be compelled depends on whether the *originals* would have been privileged or not. If the originals would not, the copies will not attract privilege just because they are part of a set of instructions to enable the client to obtain legal advice (*Dubai Bank v Galadari* [1989]).

Legal professional privilege will not protect a communication to facilitate crime or fraud (*R v Cox and Railton* [1884]; s 10(2) of PACE). 'Fraud' is very widely defined to include, in addition to the tort of deceit, 'all forms of fraud and dishonesty such as fraudulent breach of contract, fraudulent conspiracy, trickery and sham contrivances' (*Crescent Farm (Sidcup) Sports Ltd v Sterling Offices Ltd* [1972], *per* Goff J). This exception to the scope of legal professional privilege has more recently been expressed by saying that, for the privilege to apply, there must be 'absence of iniquity' (*Ventouris v Mountain* [1991], *per* Bingham LJ). In *Barclays Bank v Eustice* [1995], 'iniquity' was held to include obtaining advice about how to structure a series of transactions at an undervalue that would have had the effect of prejudicing the interests of creditors. The Court of Appeal held that it made no difference that neither the solicitor nor even the client realised that this would be the effect of what was proposed.

Criminal or fraudulent conduct undertaken by investigative agents employed by solicitors in the conduct of litigation will also cause the privilege to be lost (*Dubai Aluminium Co Ltd v Al Alawi* [1999]).

Experts' reports that are to be used at trial will have to be disclosed to the other party but one party may obtain a report that he later decides not to use. Such a report will normally be covered by legal professional privilege. However, there are two exceptions to this rule:

- reports from experts, such as doctors and psychiatrists, brought into existence by parties to cases involving the welfare of children. The overriding duty to regard the welfare of a child as paramount in such cases will not allow the parties to suppress 'unfavourable' reports (*Oxfordshire CC v M* [1994]);

■ where an expert in his report refers to material that was supplied to him for the purpose of obtaining his opinion, any privilege attaching to that material will be waived when the expert's report is served on the other party. It makes no difference that the expert might have found the material unhelpful or irrelevant (*Clough v Tameside and Glossop HA* [1998]).

DURATION OF PRIVILEGE

The general rule is, 'Once privileged, always privileged' (*Calcraft v Guest* [1898], *per* Lindley MR). So, documents prepared for one action will continue to be privileged in subsequent litigation, even though the subject matter or the parties may be different. See, for example, *The Aegis Blaze* [1986]. Another example of the maxim is the rule whereby documents concerning property rights that are privileged in the hands of one owner are privileged in the hands of that person's successors in title (*Minet v Morgan* [1873]).

It used to be thought that, where the holder of a privilege could derive no further benefit from its exercise, the privilege could be defeated by the interest of another person who needed to have access to the information, particularly where this was needed to defeat a criminal charge. However, since the decision of the House of Lords in *R v Derby Magistrates ex p B* [1995], it is clear that this is not the case. The House of Lords said there that earlier decisions to the contrary had been wrong. It is a fundamental condition, on which the administration of justice rests, that a client must be sure that what he tells his lawyer will never be revealed without consent. Otherwise, the client might hold back half the truth.

DOES THE PRIVILEGE APPLY TO ALL PARTIES AND TO ALL TYPES OF COMMUNICATIONS?

In relation to communications between a party to negotiations and a third party, the privilege only applies to admissions (*Murrell v Healey* [2001]). However, in respect of the parties to the negotiations, the privilege applies to all communications between the parties and not merely to admissions (*Unilever plc v Proctor & Gamble* [1999]). (See also: *R v Devani (Maya)* [2007]; and *R v Hall-Chung* [2007] where it was decided that despite there being a waiver of legal professional privilege between the defendant and his solicitor, there was no unfairness as he had exercised his right to silence during interview.)

BYPASSING THE PRIVILEGE VIA SECONDARY EVIDENCE

Legal professional privilege prevents facts *from having to be disclosed*. It does not prevent the facts *from being proved* if any other means of doing so can be found. Thus, in *Calcraft v Guest* [1898], where the appellant had obtained copies of certain privileged documents and so was in a position to prove the contents of the originals by means of secondary evidence, the Court of Appeal held that he was entitled to do so.

In civil proceedings, r 31.20 of the Civil Procedure Rules 1998 (CPR) provides that 'inadvertently disclosed privileged documents may only be used with the consent of the court'. It is likely that courts will be guided by earlier decisions in cases where the use of privileged documents was restrained by injunction, so some knowledge of earlier decisions will be helpful. In particular, it was held before the CPR came into force that, where a privileged document had been inadvertently disclosed, the privilege would not be lost if a reasonable person seeing it would have realised that it could only have been disclosed in error (see also *Pizzey v Ford Motor Co Ltd* [1993]; *IBM Corp v Phoenix (International) Computers Ltd* [1995]). Where a privileged document has been disclosed by misconduct, or has been obtained by malpractice, the old law presumably applies. It will be necessary to obtain an injunction (albeit in the same proceedings) restraining the use of that document. In the leading case that established this right, *Ashburton v Pape* [1913], the injunction was granted on the basis of the court's power to protect confidentiality. However, in *Goddard v Nationwide Building Society* [1986], Nourse LJ took the view that the basis of the relief was not the confidential nature of the communication, but the legal professional privilege attached to it. The importance of this distinction may lie in the fact that, on the more recent view, there appears to be less scope for a judge to exercise his discretion when deciding whether to grant the injunction (*Derby and Co Ltd v Weldon (No 8)* [1990]).

In *Butler v Board of Trade* [1971], it was held that public policy would prevent an injunction of this kind from being granted where its effect would be to restrain the prosecution from adducing admissible evidence in criminal proceedings and, in a case where the prosecution obtained a privileged communication by accident rather than impropriety, the Court of Appeal held that it could be used during the cross-examination of the defendant (*R v Tompkins* [1977]).

WAIVER AND STATUTORY ABROGATION

The client may waiver the privilege either expressly or impliedly (*British American Tobacco (Investments Ltd) v USA* [2004]). The document cannot be severed, and thus the waiver only applies to part of the communication, unless the severed part deals with a distinct subject-matter (*Great Atlantic Insurance v Home Insurance* [1981]). Legal professional privilege can also be abrogated by statute (*R (on the application of Morgan Grenfell & Co Ltd) v Special Commissioner of Income Tax* [2002]).

'WITHOUT PREJUDICE' STATEMENTS

This head of privilege is founded on the public policy of encouraging litigants to settle their differences. The rule applies to exclude from evidence all negotiations genuinely aimed at settlement, whether oral or in writing. Such statements are 'without prejudice' to their makers if the terms proposed are not accepted. The application of the rule does not depend on the use of the expression 'without prejudice', though it is safer to use it. If the circumstances make it clear that the parties were trying to settle a claim, evidence of the negotiations will not generally be admissible to establish an admission (*Ofulue and Ofulue v Bossert* [2008]). Conversely, the use of the 'without prejudice' label will be of no effect where there is no attempt at settlement (*Re Daintrey ex p Holt* [1893]).

Evidence of negotiations will be admissible if it is necessary to show the terms of a settlement that were ultimately reached: for example, where one of the parties wants to sue on that agreement (*Tomlin v Standard Telephones and Cables Ltd* [1969]), but, generally, the 'without prejudice' rule makes evidence of negotiations inadmissible in any subsequent litigation connected with the same subject matter, even where the parties are not identical (*Rush & Tomkins Ltd v GLC* [1989]).

PUBLIC INTEREST IMMUNITY

Public interest immunity (PII), formerly called 'Crown privilege', is a rule of law that requires the withholding of documents on the ground that it would be harmful to the public interest to disclose them.

In *Duncan v Cammell Laird and Co Ltd* [1942], the House of Lords held that a court could not question a claim of Crown privilege, if made in proper form. It also said that claims to Crown privilege could be put on two alternative grounds:

- disclosure of the contents of the particular documents would harm the public interest, for example, by endangering national security or prejudicing diplomatic relations (*Buttes Oil Co V Hammer (No 3)* [1981]);

- the documents belonged to a class of documents that had to be withheld in the interests of 'the proper functioning of the public service'.

In 1956, Viscount Kilmuir LC, in a statement in the House of Lords, explained that the reason for claiming Crown privilege on a class, as opposed to a contents, basis was that it was needed to secure 'freedom and candour of communications with and within the public service', so that government decisions could be taken on the best advice and with the fullest information. People advising the Government must be able to know that they were doing so in confidence and that any document containing their advice would not subsequently be disclosed.

The beginning of the modern approach to PII can be seen in *Conway v Rimmer* [1968], in which the House of Lords reversed its earlier ruling in *Duncan v Cammell Laird* and held that, in such cases, it was for the court to decide where the balance of public interest lay: in protecting a government claim for secrecy or in upholding a litigant's right to have all relevant materials available for the proper adjudication of his claim. However, the idea that PII might be based on a class, rather than a contents, claim was still accepted.

PII can operate in cases not involving the Government. In *R v Lewes JJ ex p Secretary of State for the Home Department* [1973], it was said that the old expression, 'Crown privilege', was wrong and misleading. While a minister was always an appropriate, and often the most appropriate, person to assert the public interest, it was open to any person to raise the issue, and there might be cases where the trial judge himself should do so. So, for example, in *D v NSPCC* [1978], the House of Lords protected the anonymity of an informer who had reported suspicions of child cruelty to the NSPCC.

An important distinction between PII and the sort of privilege that might be claimed by a private litigant, such as legal professional privilege or the privilege against self-incrimination, used to be that a privilege might be waived but a claim to PII could not (see, eg, *Makanjuola v Commissioner of Metropolitan Police* [1992], *per* Bingham LJ). This approach, coupled with a class claim rather than a contents claim, led to undesirably wide PII claims being made by ministers in a number of trials. The practice was criticised in the Scott Report (1996) and the Government has now effectively abandoned class claims. In *R v Chief Constable of West Midlands ex p Wiley* [1995], the House of Lords held that a class claim cannot be made in respect of documents compiled as part of the investigation of a complaint against the police.

In the last few decades, the leading cases on PII in the House of Lords were concerned with civil claims, but more recently there has been a preponderance of criminal litigation involving the rule. The basic rule is that, in public prosecutions, witnesses may not be asked, and will not be allowed to disclose, the names of informers or the nature of the information given.

The reason for the rule is that informers need to be protected, both for their own safety and to ensure that the supply of information about criminal activities does not dry up (*Marks v Beyfus* [1890]). This rule can be departed from if the disclosure of the name of the informant was necessary to show the defendant's innocence, but it is for the defendant to show that there is a good reason for disclosure (*R v Hennessey* [1978]). (See also *R v Dawson* [2007].)

▶ R v DAWSON [2007]

Basic facts

A surveillance operation had taken place which led to the defendant being convicted of six convictions for conspiracy to supply Class A and Class B drugs. The defendant made an application for the proceedings to be stayed on the basis of entrapment, but the Crown Prosecution Service held material which was protected by the public immunity test which disproved what the defendant had said in his statement. The trial judge ordered that a synopsis of this material be made available without revealing the source. After reading this he ruled that it was unnecessary for the source to be revealed.

Relevance

This decision was appealed on various grounds but the Court of Appeal ruled that had the trial proceeded, the protected material

> would have remained protected and would not have been available for the defendant nor the jury to see as there was nothing in that information which served to exculpate the defendant.

The rule in *Marks v Beyfus* also protects the identity of persons who have allowed their premises to be used for police observation, as well as the identity of the premises from which observation was kept. Even if the defendant argues that identification of the premises is necessary to establish his innocence (because, for example, it has a bearing on the accuracy of witness observations), the judge may still refuse to allow the question to be put (*R v Johnson* [1989]). The prosecution must first provide a proper evidential basis to support their claim for protection of identity. In *R v Johnson*, Watkins LJ stated the following as minimum requirements:

- the police officer in charge of the observations must testify that he visited all the observation places to be used and ascertained the attitude of their occupiers, both as to the use to be made of them and to possible subsequent disclosure;

- a police officer of at least the rank of chief inspector must testify that, immediately prior to the trial, he visited the places used for observation and ascertained whether the occupiers were the same as when the observation took place and, whether they were or not, the attitude of those occupiers to possible disclosure of their premises as observation points.

The object of keeping the identity of premises secret is to protect the owner or occupier. Where this consideration does not apply, cross-examination may be permitted on the details of surveillance (*R v Brown* [1987]).

A police informer may voluntarily sacrifice his anonymity, and PII cannot be used to prevent this (*Savage v Chief Constable of Hampshire* [1997]).

CRIMINAL PROCEDURE RULES 2005

The prosecution may seek to claim public interest immunity at an *ex parte* hearing without notifying the defence. This is appropriate where the fact that an application is being made would in itself reveal to the defence the information to which the public interest immunity claim relates. In *R v H and C* [2008] the House of Lords opined that 'There will be very few cases indeed in which some measure of disclosure to the defence will not be possible, even if this is confined to the fact that an *ex parte* application is to be made. If even that information is withheld and if the material to be withheld is of significant help to the defendant, there must be a very serious question whether the prosecution should proceed, since special counsel, even if appointed, cannot then receive any instructions from the defence at all.'

The prosecution may seek to claim public interest immunity at an *ex parte* hearing, having notified the defence that an application is being made. This procedure is appropriate where revealing the nature of the relevant material would reveal to the defence the information to which the public interest immunity claim relates. Or finally, the prosecution may seek to claim public interest immunity at an *inter partes* hearing, having notified the defence of the nature of the material. Note, however, where the prosecution seeks to claim public interest immunity by way of one of the procedures described above, the court can direct the prosecution to adopt an alternative procedure. The House of Lords established guidelines for the disclosure process in *R v H and C* [2008]. There is a very high duty on the government to provide 'full and accurate' explanations of all the facts relevant to the issue that the court must decide (*R (Quark Fishing) v Secretary of State for Foreign and Commonwealth Affairs* [2002]; *R (on application of Al-Sweady) v Secretary of State for Defence* [2009]).

You should now be confident that you would be able to tick all of the boxes on the checklist at the beginning of this chapter. To check your knowledge of Privilege and public interest immunity why not visit the companion website and take the Multiple Choice Question test. Check your understanding of the terms and vocabulary used in this chapter with the flashcard glossary.

12

Putting it into practice . . .

Now that you've mastered the basics, you will want to put it all into practice. The Routledge Questions and Answers series provides an ideal opportunity for you to apply your understanding and knowledge of the law and to hone your essay-writing technique.

We've included one exam-style essay question, reproduced from the Routledge Questions and Answers series to give you some essential exam practice. The Q & A includes an answer plan and a fully worked model answer to help you recognise what examiners might look for in your answer.

QUESTION 1

Is a concept of legal relevance useful in the law of evidence?

Answer plan

Begin by setting out the two different ways in which a legal concept can be 'useful': one is connected with what the law is, the other with what it ought to be. The question raises a classic problem on which the two great American writers on evidence, Thayer and Wigmore, had different views; these are outlined. Note that there are some cases where judges do appear to have laid down rules about what is or is not relevant and at least one occasion where Parliament has tried to do so. Note also the practice of the courts of rejecting evidence of only minimal weight on the ground that it is 'irrelevant'. But, the point is then made that none of this justifies acknowledging a concept of 'legal relevance' in existing law because:

■ such a concept would be impossible to define; and

■ it would be difficult to develop a body of case law on the subject.

In addition, such a concept would be undesirable because:

■ if a body of case law could after all be developed, it would be cumbersome and restrictive;

■ it would make it even more difficult than it is at present for the law to respond to changing conditions.

In summary, therefore, the essay is constructed as follows:

■ two ways in which a legal concept can be 'useful';

■ outline of the argument to be put forward;

■ Thayer's rejection of 'legal relevance';

■ Wigmore's contrary view;

■ judicial decisions about relevance, for example, *DPP v Camplin* [1978]; *DPP v Majewski* [1977];

■ the connection made by courts between relevance and weight;

■ apparent 'rules' about relevance: *Grant* [1996]; *Halpin* [1996]; *Guney* [1998];

■ difficulties presented by 'legal relevance'.

ANSWER

A legal concept may be useful either because it helps us to understand the law as it is, or because if it were to be introduced, it would improve the state of the law. I shall argue that a concept of legal relevance is scarcely to be found in the existing state of the law and that it would not be useful to introduce it.

Thayer defined the law of evidence as 'a set of rules and principles affecting judicial investigations into questions of fact', but he pointed out that these rules and principles do not regulate the process of reasoning, save to the extent of helping to select the factual material upon which the processes of reasoning are to operate. Chiefly, in addition to prescribing the manner of presenting evidence and fixing the qualifications and privileges of witnesses, these rules and principles determine what classes of things shall not be received in evidence. There is one principle of exclusion, however, which Thayer described as not so much a rule of evidence as a presupposition involved in the very conception of a rational system of evidence: this was the principle which forbids receiving anything irrelevant. But the law, according to Thayer, furnishes no test of relevance. For this, it tacitly refers to logic and general experience, the principles of which are presumed to be known.

Wigmore, on the other hand, questioned the idea that the law furnished no test of relevance. He argued that although relevance is originally a matter of logic and common sense, there are still many instances in which the evidence of particular facts as bearing on particular issues has been so often the subject of discussion in courts of law, and so often ruled upon, that the united logic of a great many judges and lawyers may be said to furnish evidence of the sense common to a great many individuals, and so to acquire the authority of law. It is thus proper, he argued, to talk of legal relevance.

It is certainly the case that in some instances, judges have laid down rules about what is relevant or irrelevant. For example, they have decided that age and sex are always relevant when considering the defence of provocation (*DPP v Camplin* [1978]). And intoxication is, as a matter of law, irrelevant in considering whether the *mens rea* for a crime of basic intent was present (*DPP v Majewski* [1977]). And in s 41 of the Youth Justice and Criminal Evidence Act 1999, Parliament attempted to lay down what the government minister in the House of Lords referred to as 'a statutory framework for determining relevance' in trials where a sexual offence is alleged.

But, apart from specific rules such as these, it is necessary to take into account the practice of the courts of rejecting evidence that has minimal weight on the ground that it is 'irrelevant'. Is this because the evidence falls short of the minimum requirement of something which can be called 'legal relevance'? There are good reasons why data of very slight weight should be excluded. Doing justice according to law is not the same as doing a piece of historical research. Concessions have to be made to what Justice Holmes referred to as 'the shortness of life', as well as to the financial resources of the litigants or the legal aid fund. Moreover, if the field of judicial inquiry were too wide, it might make decisions more unreliable because a mass of evidence would more readily lead to confusion.

It is also possible for the courts to develop something that can appear at first glance to be a rule about relevance in a particular type of situation, but which is really something else. Over the last few years, there has been a cluster of cases concerned with the precise significance to be attached to the discovery of large sums of cash in the possession of persons charged with possession of drugs with intent to supply. In one of these cases, *Grant* [1996], it was said in the Court of Appeal that if there was any possible reason other than drug dealing for the defendant's possession of cash, the finding of the cash was to be treated as irrelevant, and juries should be so directed. And, in *Halpin* [1996], the Court of Appeal said that evidence of a defendant's possession of large amounts of money, or of his extravagant lifestyle, could not be relevant where the issue in the case was possession, rather than intent to supply. However, this was later rejected in *Guney* [1998], where the Court of Appeal said that although evidence of cash or lifestyle might only rarely be relevant where there was a charge of simple possession of drugs, such evidence could not be excluded as irrelevant as a matter of law. The relevance of any item of evidence is to be decided 'not on abstract legal theory but on the circumstances of each individual case' (see also *Griffiths* [1998]). It appears that the courts, at any rate, are reluctant to acknowledge a concept of 'legal relevance', higher and stricter than logical relevance. In fact, two main difficulties lie in the way of such development.

The first is that a concept of this kind would defy definition. The second is that since each case would be decided on its own facts, there would be considerable difficulty in developing a body of case law about what was legally relevant. The examples cited earlier of *DPP v Camplin* and *DPP v Majewski* are better seen as defining the substantive law in relation to particular offences than in saying something about a concept called 'legal relevance'.

Not only does there seem to be little support for the proposition that a concept of legal relevance – despite the language of some judges – can be found in the law; there appear to be good reasons why such a concept should not be recognised.

In the first place, there is an inherent conflict between a theory that all logically relevant evidence should be admitted unless excluded by a clear ground of policy, and a theory of legal relevance, which would require a minimum quantity of probative value for each item of evidence in any particular case. There is a danger that a concept of legal relevance, if consistently applied, would exclude logically relevant evidence unless legal precedent authorised its admission. If, despite difficulties, a body of case law were to develop, it would give rise to a large number of cumbersome rules and exceptions. The second reason why a concept of legal relevance ought not to be recognised is that to fix relevance in a straitjacket of case law would make it even more difficult than it already is to adapt the law to changing circumstances.

Necessarily, judges' decisions about relevance reflect the prevailing value judgments of the society in which they live. Relevance can become a useful instrument for discarding arguments and evidence that challenge important, though perhaps unexpressed, values. Thus, in the 19th century, the courts upheld a notion of freedom of contract which allowed them to argue that an aggrieved worker could have protected his position by insisting on an appropriate contractual stipulation. Evidence of inequality of bargaining power would have been ruled 'irrelevant'. That what is relevant depends on the basic assumptions of a particular society becomes even clearer when one considers the evidential significance of marks on the bodies of those formerly suspected of witchcraft, or of the appearance in their vicinity of such creatures as a cat, a toad or a wasp.

No one, of course, could argue a case from a standpoint wholly outside the beliefs of his own society. And it may well be that arguments about relevance will be constrained by the way in which the substantive law is defined. What one can reasonably hope is that the ability to argue from a critical standpoint in particular cases should not be easily frustrated. A further obstacle in the way of such arguments would be likely to emerge if a concept of legal relevance were to become fully developed in the law of evidence.

A concept of legal relevance could also lead to unfairness to defendants, who might be prevented from adducing relevant and weighty evidence in support of their defence. This was recognised, in effect, by the House of Lords in *A* [2001], when the law lords interpreted s 41 of the Youth Justice and Criminal Evidence Act 1999 in the light of the Human Rights Act 1998 and the defendant's right to a fair trial under Article 6 of the European Convention on Human Rights.

Each Routledge Q & A contains 50 essay and problem-based questions on topics commonly found on exam papers, complete with answer plans and fully worked model answers. For further examination practice, visit the Routledge website or your local bookstore today!

ROUTLEDGE LAWCARDS

are your complete, up-to-date pocket-sized guides to key examinable areas of the undergraduate law curriculum and the CPE/GDL.

New editions of all titles in the series are publishing in February 2010.

Commercial Law 2010-2011
Company Law 2010-2011
Constitutional & Administrative Law 2010-2011
Contract Law 2010-2011
Criminal Law 2010-2011
Employment Law 2010-2011
English Legal System 2010-2011
European Union Law 2010-2011
Evidence 2010-2011
Family Law 2010-2011
Human Rights Law 2010-2011
Intellectual Property Law 2010-2011
Jurisprudence 2010-2011
Land Law 2010-2011
Tort Law 2010-2011
Equity & Trusts 2010-2011

For a full listing, visit:
www.routledgelaw.com/revisionaids.asp

Routledge
Taylor & Francis Group

ROUTLEDGE Q&A SERIES

Each Routledge Q&A contains 50 questions on topics commonly found on exam papers, with comprehensive suggested answers. The titles are written by lecturers who are also examiners, so the student gains an important insight into exactly what examiners are looking for in an answer. This makes them excellent revision and practice guides.

Titles in the series include:
Business Law
Civil Liberties & Human Rights
Company Law
Commercial Law
Constitutional & Administrative Law
Contract Law
Criminal Law
Employment Law
English Legal System
Equity & Trusts
European Union Law
Evidence
Family Law
Intellectual Property Law
Jurisprudence
Land Law
Torts

For a full listing, visit:
www.routledgelaw.com/revisionaids.asp